IN QUEST OF FREEDOM

About the Author

James Fernandes was born in Goa in 1933, and spent his childhood and boyhood in the village of Assonora. He joined the Goan freedom movement sometime after completing his school studies. In March 1955 he was arrested and sentenced to twelve years of imprisonment. He spent a period of four years and five months in Portuguese jails, most of it in Aguada Fort Prison. After his release he went to Bombay and resumed college studies. For the past twenty-three years he has been teaching English literature in St. Xavier's College, Mapusa. He lives with his wife and five children in Assonora. Since the liberation of Goa he has kept himself aloof from all politics, confining his interest to reading, teaching and a little farming.

IN QUEST OF FREEDOM

JAMES FERNANDES

CONCEPT PUBLISHING COMPANY PVT. LTD.
NEW DELHI-110059

The Xavier Centre of Historical Research (Goa) has sponsored the publication of this book. However, the responsibility for the contents of the book — facts, opinions, material used, etc. — is entirely the authors and not of the Xavier Centre for Historical Research (Goa)

ISBN-13: 978-81-7022-309-2

Edition 2016

Published and Printed by

Concept Publishing Company Pvt. Ltd.
A/15-16, Commercial Block, Mohan Garden
New Delhi-110059 (India)
T: 25351460, 25351794, *F*: 091-11-25357109
E: publishing@conceptpub.com, W: www.conceptpub.com
Editorial Office: H-13, Bali Nagar, New Delhi-110 015, India.

Cataloging in Publication Data--Courtesy: D.K. Agencies (P) Ltd. <docinfo@dkagencies.com>

Fernandes, James, 1933- author.
In quest of freedom / James Fernandes.
pages cm
Autobiographical account of a freedom fighter in the liberation of Goa, India.
Includes index.
ISBN 9788170223092

1. Fernandes, James, 1933- 2. Nationalists--India--Goa (State)--Biography. 3. Nationalism--India--Goa (State)--History. 4. Goa (India : State)--Politics and government. I. Xavier Centre of Historical Research. II. Title.

DS498.7.F47 2016 DDC 320.954799 23

Dedicated to
all Goan Patriots who
walked in the footsteps
of Gandhi

CONTENTS

PREFACE

The freedom struggle which began in 1954 and which led to Goa's liberation in 1961 is one of the most important events in the last four and a half centuries of Goa's history. But it is an event which in the context of today's rapid changes seems to be fast receding into the past, and the present young generation of Goans may not know much about it, particularly about the human aspect of the freedom struggle – an aspect which often is unavailable in historical accounts, and so remains largely unknown. What I mean by its human aspect is the event as it was experienced and lived through by those who participated in it, and even by others who were in any way affected by it. I feel that accounts of the Goan freedom movement representing the personal experiences of freedom fighters could re–create that period and bring back to life those exciting times of the freedom struggle.

It was my close contact with the young generation, in my capacity as a college teacher, that made me aware of the need of accounts dealing with this human side of the freedom struggle; and the present book is a modest attempt to meet that need. In truth, the idea of the kind of account I would write took shape under the keen interest of students who wanted me to share with them my experiences of the struggle. This account as it deals only with my personal experiences does not pretend to be a full story of the struggle; but, it is hoped, it may enable the reader to form a good idea of what hundreds of freedom fighters who waged the non-violent struggle have gone through.

The days of the freedom struggle were times of great experiences, times when we dared difficult tasks, when we faced dangers, but felt ourselves to be fully alive. Succeeding generations of Goans will not see such days, will not be called upon to go through the ordeals we went through. So memories of those great times, specially memories of the experiences of those who suffered to bring freedom to Goa have to be kept alive for the benefit of the coming generations. In this regard those of us who had the good fortune to be young when we joined the freedom movement, and so felt everything about the struggle all the more intensely, can share many valuable experiences with the young generation – our patriotism which inspired us to action; our idealism which sustained us through the hard struggle and through the long, dreary years of imprisonment; our adventure in undertaking the perilous journeys by night to attend nationalist meetings across the Goa border; our hardships while working for the movement outside, and our sufferings while languishing in jail; our sense of exhilaration as the movement rose to its climax and the goal of freedom seemed to lie within reach, and our sense of frustration as the movement weakened and the goal seemed to recede.

I myself find it amazing in retrospect, that in those stormy times hundreds of Goans, particularly young Goans could leave everything behind and plunge into the struggle when the least we could expect was spending years of our youthful life in jail. Like young people of all times we also had an urge for self-fulfilment; but as we loved our land, and our land then demanded sacrifices, we had to make our self-fulfilment a part of our yearning for a better future for Goa.

Our participation in the freedom movement has had a transforming influence on our life. The satisfaction that comes from participation in a successful national struggle is a pure joy that can be known only by a true patriot, and we have experienced that joy. We have also had the satisfaction that comes from transcending the narrow limits of one's personality by losing oneself in something greater than oneself, in a great cause, in a great movement, by being part of a great historical event. And how significant the event when placed in its wider historical perspective! This event ended the last foreign rule on Indian soil – a foreign rule that had seemed to be eternal because it had outlived the rise and fall of two successive, mighty, and long-lasting empires in India; it had established itself before the great Moghul empire had risen, and it still seemed to be going strong years after the glorious British empire had vanished. And to think that in the four and half centuries of its long duration, it was the proud privilege of my generation of Goans to have risen against it, waged an arduous struggle against it, and helped to end it. Previous generations did not see the light of freedom. Succeeding generations will have freedom, but will not get the thrill of fighting for it. We have been fortunate to have lived at the crossroads of history and experienced both.

And finally the peculiar satisfaction that comes from going through a great ordeal without cracking up or without losing one's humanity. This satisfaction has not much to do with the success or failure of the struggle. It arises from the conviction that "the struggle availeth", from a willing acceptance of the hardships and sufferings of the struggle, and from keeping oneself open to their healing powers. A long period of imprisonment is a rigorous test of a man's powers of endurance. It can break his spirit even to the extent of rendering him a physical and mental wreck, or it can make him mentally more resilient. It can fill his soul with bitterness, ill-will and hatred, or it can reinforce his humanity by making him kinder, more generous, more compassionate.

I am glad to say that most of us came through the ordeal creditably, with our humanity intact. So much so that when I think of some particular instances of our harsh treatment by our former 'enemies', I do not find myself harbouring any animosity towards them. We are now able to view the struggle itself in a different light. It now appears as a clash of two great impersonal forces – forces which transcend human wills, but which take possession of individuals and move them; and it appears that we freedom fighters, on our side, merely acted our parts, just as those whom fate had pitted against us as our 'enemies', acted theirs. Hence no reason remains for hatred or bitterness.

The struggle has really been worth all our troubles. And the young generation may find the story of that struggle interesting, and in certain ways even inspiring, particularly when they remember that the freedom which they inherit has issued from that struggle.

I wonder whether it would have been better to write this account in some other form so that my person did not figure so conspicuously in the narrative, and obtrude so much on the reader's attention. But perhaps it cannot be helped, as in any other form, the intimacy and the authenticity of the impressions sought to be conveyed here would suffer. However, I would like to emphasize that most of my experiences presented here are not entirely unusual, or peculiar to me alone, that in fact they are representative of the experiences of hundreds of freedom fighters who worked for the non-violent movement, and courted and suffered years of imprisonment. The reader can imagine each one of them having a similar story to tell.

In bringing forth this little work, I also cherish the hope that this account may serve to dispel certain misconceptions about freedom fighters in general, prevalent in the minds of a number of Goans. It is supposed that self-interest motivated most of the freedom fighters, that political ambitions prompted them to join the struggle. I hope this account will help to convey the truth that it is not self-interest alone which moves people, that patriotism and idealism also do impel people to great action. I may also add, there have been hundreds of freedom fighters like me, who after liberation, have been content to attend to their personal life, already disrupted by the struggle, and have not cared to pursue any political career. There were a number of senior freedom fighters, however, who, feeling that their responsibility did not end with the attainment of freedom sought to serve this territory, even after liberation, by trying to provide political leadership to the Goan people. With their background of sacrifices and their proven spirit of service, most of these men were more suited for the role of political leadership than the upstart and self-seeking sectarian politicians that came to supplant them; and given the opportunity these freedom fighters might have served Goa admirably. But, as clarified at the end of this account, the unfortunate circumstances that came to prevail in Goa soon after liberation, did not permit them to remain politically active for long.

James Fernandes

ACKNOWLEDGEMENTS

I am grateful to Rev. Dr. Teotonio R. de Souza, S.J., Director of the Xavier Centre of Historical Research (Goa), for undertaking to publish this little work relating to the Goan freedom struggle. I was emboldened to approach the Xavier Centre for help when Dr. de Souza organized a seminar on Oral History of Goa's freedom struggle some years ago. That was a proof of the interest of this Institute in promoting research in the patriotic struggle of the Goans. In addition, I am indebted to Dr. de Souza for certain valuable suggestions intended to enhance the historical worth of the book, which was written primarily as an account of my personal experiences.

I must record my gratitude to Shri Robert Mendonça-Kamat, the Managing Director of Lawrence & Mayo (Bombay), my co-villager and boyhood friend for his generous offer to provide financial assistance to publish this book.

My thanks are also due to my colleagues at St. Xavier's College (Mapusa, Goa), Prof. Anne Menezes, Fr. Eufemiano Miranda, Prof. Newman Fernandes and Prof. Daniel D'Souza for encouraging me to write, for correcting the drafts. and for offering various suggestions to improve the work.

Finally, my very special thanks to my student Mr. Jude Fernandes, who patiently typed the manuscript, foregoing other youthful diversions, all out of regard for a teacher.

James Fernandes

1

PRELUDE

In the course of four and a half centuries of Goa's colonial subjection there had been from time to time various revolts against Portuguese rule by different sections of the Goan people. However, none of those revolts had in its dimensions and its strength approached the great struggle of 1954 – not even the movement of 1946 which, being a spontaneous popular outburst occasioned by the visit of the Indian leader Lohia, to Goa, was more in the nature of a civil disobedience movement, and was largely confined to South Goa, particularly to the town of Margão. The freedom movement of 1954, was, by contrast, a planned, determined and sustained struggle waged over a number of years by the Goan people in general – a struggle which created the conditions for, and which had as its necessary conclusion, the liberation of Goa in 1961.

The 1954 struggle developed into a powerful people's movement because of the following new factors which by then had made their appearance in relation to the Goa political scene, and which favourably affected the freedom movement : (1) Encouraged by the stir caused by Lohia in 1946, most of the Goan patriots had united to establish the first great patriotic organisation of Goans – the National Congress (Goa) which laid the groundwork and launched the non-violent struggle in 1954, and further directed its operations all through its course. (2) By 1954 the world situation was rapidly changing: the forces of colonialism were in many parts of the world in full retreat. Hence Goan patriots waged their struggle, with the confidence that History was on their side. (3) In this movement, Goans did not feel themselves alone in their fight against a mighty power, as they now had the backing of an independent India. In truth most Goan patriots, though they accepted their responsibility to launch the movement, now considered the freedom of Goa a problem of not Goans alone, but of all Indians too.

Amidst wide publicity, the movement was launched from Indian territory on 15th August, the day of Independence, with the dispatch initially of three batches of Goan *satyagrahis* to enter Goa from three different directions. Hundreds of Indian volunteers had prepared themselves to accompany the Goan *satyagrahis* into Goa; but the Government of India, in order to give the lie to the Portuguese propaganda that Goans were not interested in freedom, intervened and prevented Indian *satyagrahis* from crossing over into Goa, leaving the Goans to carry on the struggle on their own, and thus to make their will known to the world, before they could expect assistance from the people and the Government of India. After 15th of August, the scene of most nationalist activity shifted to Goa with scores of National Congress (Goa) workers moving secretly among the people, spreading the message of freedom by word of mouth and printed matter, enrolling fresh N.C.(G.) members, organizing cells of workers in various towns and villages of Goa, and preparing groups of patriots to offer *satyagraha* on different historic occasions. And as a result of the efforts of all these workers, the freedom movement spread to every nook and corner of Goa, drawing into the struggle people from all walks of life -- farmers and artisans, clerks and merchants, students and teachers, lawyers and doctors. Leaflets and posters appeared in every part of Goa demanding the end of Portuguese rule; people began to offer *satyagraha* and court imprisonment; arrests of nationalists went on increasing; and jails in Goa began to fill up.

To deal with the people's agitation the government brought more and more contingents of police and military forces from Portugal, with the result that white men in uniform began to appear everywhere in Goa, making still more flagrant the oppressive nature of the colonial regime, and highlighting the Goans' status as a subject people.

2

I PREPARE TO PLUNGE INTO THE STRUGGLE

Young Goans with a little sense of patriotism could not remain indifferent spectators to the situation in Goa as it developed particularly after August, 1954. And there were many Goans like me who loved their country in their own quiet way and who now awoke to their responsibility to their motherland.

How did I learn to love my land? In the very process of growing up, I suppose. I believe that a man who is a little sensitive and has some sense of dignity is naturally a patriot. He not only feels a sense of kinship with the people born and bred in the land, but he also loves the very soil of the land, its hills and fields, its mountains and valleys, its streams and rivers. To such a man, there is something galling in the sight of an alien people coming into his land and strutting about as its masters. Such a man, I believe, is prepared to undergo a little suffering for the love of his land.

My patriotism was further nurtured by some of the great books I read in early life. Among those books which had a great impact on my young mind, I may mention Nehru's *Discovery of India* and H.G.Wells's *The Outline of History*. These books revealed to me the unique civilization that India has had – a civilization based not so much on military strength, but on things of the human spirit. I still remember, for instance, the thrill with which I read H.G.Wells's account (the closing words particularly) of the achievement of King Asoka (third century B.C.) who renounced war after victory, out of revulsion at its bloodshed and established an empire of peace and benevolence: "Amidst the tens of thousands of names of monarchs that crowd the columns of history... the name of Asoka shines, and shines almost alone, a star." These books widened my mental horizons and supplied a basis for my legitimate pride as an Indian. From the historical perspective provided by such books it was not difficult for me to foresee the doom of Portuguese colonialism, and Goa's subsequent destiny with the rest of India.

Of course, it needed no great political foresight in the middle of the twentieth century to see the end of Portuguese colonialism, when the great British empire itself was crumbling. Educated people all over the world had by then come to realise that western colonialism together with its corollary of the superiority of western civilization was but a passing phase in the history of the world. However, not only had the Portuguese rulers developed political myopia, but surprisingly many Goans also came to regard Portuguese rule in Goa as something permanent and immutable. Some of them had unquestioningly swallowed Salazar's gimmick of calling Goa and all the other colonies "overseas provinces of Portugal." Perhaps some looked upon Portuguese rule in Goa as an exception to the law of historical change, as there was no economic exploitation of Goa by Portugal. It was contended that holding on to Goa was a matter of prestige for Portugal. But these people failed to see that what was prestige for Portugal was degradation for Goa. And, in truth, the Portuguese rulers clung on to Goa not merely for prestige, but because holding on to Goa helped them to hold on to, and exploit the large African colonies. It was mainly the English educated Goans who could see Portuguese rule in Goa from the larger historical perspective.

Though Goa enjoyed in those days the reputation of an idyllic land of peace and tranquillity, fledgelings like me eager to fly out into a wider world of opportunities, felt life in Goa cramped and stagnant. There were hardly any job opportunities, particularly for young people with English education. And for education higher than S.S.C. one had to go outside Goa. My family could not afford to send me out for higher education, and so I remained in Goa and tried my hand at some odd, unsatisfactory jobs, thereby adding to my frustration.

There were a number of other young men mooning around, not knowing what to do in life, and the sight of all these idlers further oppressed my spirit. The stagnant situation in Goa had provoked me to think, and at about that time I had arrived at the conclusion that a civilised society should be able to create adequate opportunities for the self-fulfilment of its young men and women. I could see that in

Goa such a state of affairs could come not under a colonial government, but only when Goa was free and united with the rest of the country. I remember discussing these ideas with my young friends and feeling encouraged to find that they espoused them warmly.

And then the freedom movement started. The news of the launching of the freedom struggle by the National Congress (Goa) in 1954 came as a great relief to my oppressed spirit. We had wanted to do away with a hateful regime which had compelled us to live without hope, but not knowing how to resist it we had felt ourselves powerless against it. But now a way of resisting it was open, now we could act. The launching of the struggle came like a clarion call to me, and naturally, I responded by deciding to participate in the freedom movement.

No doubt the decision to join the movement was not easy to take. Knowing the harsh, intolerant nature of the autocratic regime we were up against, I realised that the prospect we faced was long years of imprisonment, or worse. It implied, at best, long postponement of all our hopes for personal development, at worst, the complete loss of those hopes. Undoubtedly young men in Goa belonging to families with limited means generally lived without much hope. But even then one could entertain the hope of going out of Goa, finding some employment and getting some higher education. Now our only self-fulfilment lay through the crucible of the freedom struggle.

The decision had also been hard to take, and had entailed a great deal of heart-searching, particularly because of the pain my participation would cause to my family. At no time had I lived apart from them, and as usually happens with a family that goes through hardships together, we were much attached to one another. In the circumstances I could not contemplate without the greatest dismay the possibility of my being torn away from the family.

I began to consider how my family could be won over, and their consent obtained for my participation in the terrible undertaking. For some time I even toyed with the idea of carrying on the activities of the movement without the knowledge of my people. But then, I thought, if I were to be arrested suddenly, the shock might be too painful for them to bear. Somehow they had to be prepared beforehand for that great eventuality.

In the meanwhile I took steps to get in touch with workers of the National Congress (Goa). After months of discreet enquiries here and there, I managed to meet one such worker who used to make occasional secret visits to Aldona. I always remember Mohan, not only because he initiated me into the Freedom Movement, but also because he was in many respects an interesting character. I was immediately impressed by his sturdy built, his maturity (he was about 25), and his good education. He was not a Goan, but had spent a couple of years in Goa trying his luck as some building contractor. I wondered what stake he had in the freedom of Goa. Gradually I came to understand that it was not merely patriotism which had led him into the freedom struggle. He was some sort of an adventurer and the dull work of a building contractor had not been congenial to his adventurous spirit; so he had drifted into the freedom struggle. He outlined to us the strategy of the National Congress (Goa), the organisation of Goans which was committed to a non-violent struggle and which had launched the movement by sending into Goa *satyagrahis* recruited from Goans resident in Bombay. But thenceforth not many more Bombay Goans could be expected to volunteer to march into Goa, and so the N.C.(G) was going to concentrate its main efforts in Goa itself. Its plan was to enroll active members all over Goa to begin with, so that every town and village had a cell of workers who could then by enlisting people's support for the movement help to intensify it till it became a real mass movement. On special occasions the N.C. (G) workers were to organise in the various Taluka capitals demonstrations by large numbers of people with the display of posters and national flags.

Mohan informed us about the camps maintained by N.C.(G.) on the other side of Goa's frontier, at places like Majali, Kundal and Sanquirvale, where periodically meetings of workers from Goa were held. These meetings were usually addressed by Peter Alvares who had now assumed leadership of the movement. Peter Alvares was a Goan who had earned for himself a high position in Indian public life, being the President of the All-India Railwaymen's Federation and a prominent leader of the erstwhile Praja Socialist Party. Mohan told us that the next meeting was scheduled for early December at Kundal, a place across the eastern border, on the top of the Ghats overlooking Sanguem taluka; and he offered to take any one of us there as a representative of our area to meet Peter Alvares. I immediately volunteered to go with him. Then appointing a certain day to meet him in Margão, he took his leave. But before he left, he had us enrolled as members of National Congress (Goa).

The die was now finally cast and there was no turning back. What lay before us as I could see, was a long, hard struggle whose end was not in sight. That fateful day when I joined the N.C.(G), I had the feeling of standing at the edge of a dark, wide abyss which we were venturing to cross – an abyss whose remote shore was all enveloped in gloom. Only at rare hopeful moments did I seem to catch a faint glimmer of the distant shore of freedom.

Now my participation in the movement could not be kept secret from my family. For one thing, my departure for the meeting at Kundal would entail a few day's absence from home, for which I needed their consent. For another, there was just the likelihood of my being arrested while illegally crossing the frontier on the way to, or from Kundal; nay, henceforth the risk of arrest was an ever present threat. I was particularly afraid of the pain and sorrow the disclosure would cause to my aging mother; but somehow, they had to be informed. At lunch time I began by talking about the rising freedom movement. I told them of rumours of big preparations being afoot in Goa and outside to intensify the movement. I misrepresented things a bit. I told them that if the Portuguese government went on using repression after the movement reached a certain pitch, it was believed that the Government of India would take armed action and liberate Goa. I gave it as the opinion of well-informed people that Goa would be free very soon. They listened with great interest. Both were decidedly patriotic, and had enough of English education to understand that colonialism was collapsing in every part of the world. But when I told them that I was going to join the movement they were quite alarmed. I could see fear in my mother's eyes, fear about what would happen to me once I fell into the hands of the Portuguese police. I tried to reassure her by telling her that the stories of police brutalities were exaggerated. I pointed out that, anyhow, there was no future for us until Goá was free. It was only when she found me quite adamant, that she gradually resigned herself to the possibility of my going to prison. My sister was more courageous. She had always shown courage in the management of the household through all adverse circumstances. Now I derived great encouragement from her stoical acceptance of my participation in the movement and all its possible consequences. Having thus taken my people into confidence, I was now quite braced up to face all the rigours of the freedom struggle.

3

A MEETING ACROSS THE WILD GHATS

On the appointed day, early in November I travelled to Margão and met Mohan in the afternoon. He informed me that he was expecting six more workers from different parts of Goa to arrive at Margão by evening, and that early morning we could all begin the journey to Kundal. He put me up for the night with another N.C.(G) worker, a student of Portuguese Lyceum, who was also to accompany us to Kundal. Kantak, this Lyceum student was about my age, and was of a friendly, frank disposition. Our friendship which began with the adventure of crossing the wild Ghats together, was later revived and strengthened by our meeting as prisoners in jail. That evening my idealist friend talked optimistically about the outcome of the movement. And after food he took me to see the movie *War of the Worlds* based on the science fiction work of the same name by H. G. Wells, which I had read. At night, I remember, we had a lively discussion on the film – on the possibility of extraterrestrial creatures invading our earth, with my optimistic Lyceum friend emphatically maintaining the belief that alien beings, who could be intelligent enough to develop the means to reach our planet, could not at the same time be cruel enough to want to exterminate the human race and take possession of our earth. But before going to bed we left off thinking about hypothetical problems of cosmic significance, and came to the pressing problem we faced – freedom for Goa; and hoping that we would not land in jail before returning from the meeting, we dropped off to sleep.

In the morning we went to the bus-stand and met Mohan, who told us that another six people were coming with us. To ward off suspicion we did not all get together, but remained in three separate groups; and in separate groups we travelled by that old time bus, *caminhão*, which carried about twenty-five people. Our first destination was Neturli, a small village at the foot of the Ghats. Mohan had told us that Neturli was the point of maximum danger in the journey. There was no human habitation beyond Neturli to the east, and the place being a very small village, any strangers alighting from a *caminhão* and proceeding towards the Ghats and the frontier, would be quite conspicuous. And if there were any police spies around, or worse still, if we were to be surprised by a police patrol while leaving the village, we would be in a very uncomfortable position indeed! We knew, in fact, that since the beginning of the movement, police patrolling in the border areas had been intensified. Fortunately for us, some mining operations were going on at that time in the hills around Neturli, and we could pretend going towards the mines.

We arrived at Neturli in the afternoon and found it a real sleepy place. The Lyceum student and I got down first and with an air as business-like as we could affect, walked towards the dug-up hills which appeared to the south-east. As far as we could see, no inquisitive eyes watched us. After thus walking about two furlongs up the hill slopes, we glanced back and saw another of our group following us far behind. We then changed direction and struck towards the east, directly towards the imposing western Ghats. Soon we reached the safety of the thickly forested lower slopes of the Ghats, and there waited for our other companions to come up.

And then we began the arduous climb up the Ghats. In these parts the mountains were all covered with thick virgin forests through which it was difficult to find one's way, and in certain places one came to dense thickets virtually impossible to penetrate. Mohan told us that there were certain easier routes through the forest – beaten tracks used by smugglers, which we could have availed ourselves of, only on the lower reaches of the mountains, as on the upper reaches these tracks changed direction so as to give a wide berth to the Customs Post at Kundal. On an earlier occasion when he had led a batch of N.C.(G) workers up to Kundal, Mohan had taken the help of a local guide who had directed them up one such track. Now we spent half an hour searching for those tracks, but not finding any, decided to go up as best we could, taking a general easterly direction, hoping to find one as we proceeded. But those legendary paths through the forest eluded us till the end of this hard journey.

The climb was hard not so much due to the steepness of the slopes, but because we had to make our way through boulders and bushes. Now and then we came to open spaces, but mostly we had to push through the thick jungle, and hence, our progress was quite slow. The total distance we walked might have been about seven miles (though the actual distance between Neturli and Kundal as the crow flies, will be less); but we toiled up the slopes for more than four hours to cover this distance. All the same, climbing the Ghats for the first time was for me an exhilarating experience.

At dusk we reached Kundal exhausted but in high spirits. Perched on the top of the Ghats and surrounded by jungle, Kundal appears to be cut off from the world. It comprised in those days besides a *Dharamashala*, four or five small cottages one of which was used as a Customs office and the others as quarters for the Customs staff. Its only link with the outside world was the narrow mud-road which, snaking through the forest, led to Kumbarwada, a village eight miles away to the east, on the outskirts of the jungle. About once a week, we were told, a jeep coming from the outside world, via Kumbarwada, rode up the narrow jungle road, bringing provisions for the Customs people at Kundal.

There was hardly any amenity of civilization available here, and naturally most of the Customs staff as we learnt, always dreamed of transfer elsewhere. No one could be expected to like the idea of spending years or even months here, unless one had something of the hermit in one's constitution, and could be happy communing with mountains and forests.

We wondered why the N.C.(G) was maintaining a camp at such an inaccessible place as Kundal; we were told that it was considered to be a convenient venue for the meetings of workers from central and eastern Goa. But later on it was found that N.C.(G) workers preferred to attend meetings at the comparatively more accessible camps at Majali to the south-east of Goa, and Sanquirvale to the north-east, rather than climb the forbidding Ghats to reach Kundal. Nevertheless, it was a beautiful place, and the majestic mountains and the deep forests cast their peculiar spell on all sensitive natures.

One of the primitive looking cottages was a *Dharamashala* and was being utilised by N.C.(G) as its "camp". It looked a very unimpressive camp. And we, walking into that cottage, exhausted and footsore, looked more a group of pilgrims than a troop of revolutionaries. It was rather discouraging to speculate that such small, insignificant looking bands of patriots like us, meeting in such humble conditions as these N.C.(G) camps, were going to challenge the centuries-old, solidly entrenched Portuguese regime in Goa. We appeared so weak and our antagonist looked so formidable! But there was consolation in the thought that many great changes in the world had, in fact, small, inconspicuous, and humble beginnings;

that many revolutionary movements began as thin tricklets, but gradually, in the course of time, developed into mighty floods. We hoped that our Goan struggle also would gradually draw in the mass of people and would become a powerful torrent that not all the NATO-supplied arms of the Portuguese government would be able to quell.

Peter Alvares arrived at Kundal by jeep late in the evening. He ate with us the simple food prepared by our workers and then he addressed us. He did not hold out any false hopes for the immediate success of the struggle, but spelled out the long course of action that the N.C.(G) had set for itself, and of which we had been informed by Mohan. He assured us that once the movement in Goa reached its climax, we could expect to get the support of the people of entire India. He was already in touch with the leaders of various political organisations in India on this question of mobilising support of all the Indian people for the Goan struggle. We felt at that time that it was very comforting for us to have as the leader of our movement, a man who, though a Goan, had the stature of a prominent all-India political figure. Under his leadership, we felt, the Goan people were not alone.

Another purpose that these meetings across the border served was that we could get here our supply of the "propaganda material" in the form of pamphlets, leaflets, posters and flags. This material was of great use to us as a weapon of agitation. For obvious reasons, it was very difficult to prepare it all in Goa, and so it was brought across the border and passed on to N.C.(G) workers in every place. Some of the later meetings we attended at Sanquirvale were mainly with the intention of getting our supply of this material.

The next morning after the meeting we all crowded into Peter Alvares's jeep and left Kundal for Kumbarwada. Alvares was on his way to Belgaum. The other workers did not want to return to Goa by the same difficult route we had come up. They wanted to enter Goa by the southern Majali route which some of them knew. I had wished to return immediately by the same route as I had promised my family to be back home in three or four days. But Mohan who was to accompany me, wished to visit some relatives at Belgaum before returning to Goa, and requested me to wait for another day, on his account. He suggested that I spend a day and a night at Kumbarwada where my board and lodging would be arranged at the expense of the N.C.(G). Mohan was to return to Kumbarwada by noon the day after and then the two of us would walk back to Kundal.

4

A STRANGE ENCOUNTER IN THE JUNGLE

In accordance with Mohan's plan I alone halted at Kumbarwada while the others continued their journey. My board at Kumbarwada consisted of the arrangement to have two meals a day at a dingy private inn, which for me was quite satisfactory. My lodging consisted of the privilege of sleeping on a wooden bench on the open porch of a tea-stall, after the stall closed for the night – which arrangement was rather unsatisfactory, as, not having any bedsheet with me, I was fully exposed to the cold of a high-altitude place like Kumbarwada. (It was the beginning of the cold season).

I spent the first day exploring the fields and forests around the village. In the evening after sunset, I could feel the cold descending speedily upon the place. I could have asked for a blanket or bedsheet from the inn, but I was too shy to ask a favour from strangers. So I spent the night alternately lying shivering on the bench, and walking about vigorously to regain warmth, until the morning brought some comfort in the form of, first, a hot cup of tea, and then an increasingly warm sun.

Mohan was expected to arrive by noon of the second day. I spent this second day in more extensive explorations of the environs of Kumbarwada, now and then coming to the village to see whether Mohan had arrived. As he had not come by nightfall, when the last bus arrived and departed, I was beginning to feel anxious and upset. I was afraid that my prolonged absence would cause great anxiety to my family. I decided not to wait for him beyond noon of the next day. The second night I was a little better prepared to fight the cold. Collecting some inflammable rubbish, I made a fire, near which I sat and dozed for a couple of hours; and then spent the rest of the night watching the stars.

The third day I waited for Mohan with mounting anxiety; and when by lunch-time he had not come, my mind was made up. I kept a message for Mohan at the tea-stall and at the inn that I had left for Kundal from where, the next afternoon I would leave for Goa. Then after lunch I set off on the lonely road to Kundal.

A few minutes after leaving the village I entered the jungle. The distance between Kumbarwada and Kundal is eight miles, and all this distance of eight miles, there is nothing but thick jungle. So that if any mishap befell a person walking this jungle road, and he screamed for help, only God could hear him. I knew this remote jungles to be infested with various wild animals, some of them rather dangerous. Even while climbing up the Ghats, on our approach to Kundal after sunset, we had come upon a leopard sized animal slinking into the bushes. We couldn't be sure whether it was a leopard or a panther, as we did not get a clear view in the waning light. But now as I penetrated deeper into the jungle, being all alone, I began to feel a little uneasy. I felt the need to have something in the hand as a sort of weapon, and breaking a suitable branch of a little tree, I carried it as a dependable staff. This arming myself proved quite providential, as later on, when I faced an emergency, without this staff I would have felt myself quite defenceless, and might have even panicked.

As I walked on, the thick surrounding jungle seemed to cast its peculiar awesome influence. The rustling of leaves in the wind, the sound of unseen waterfalls and mountain streams from far and near, the calls of strange birds and animals – all these merged together to form a natural, wild harmony which seemed to permeate one's very being. And now and then through an opening in the dark trees I caught a glimpse of a towering mountain peak, strangely lit up by the afternoon sun.

Thus inspired with awe of the jungle, I trudged on and on, like one bewitched, without knowing how much of the distance I had covered. I neither had a watch with me to indicate how long I had walked, nor did I remember any landmark on the way, except the stream which cut across the road, and that was very near Kundal (We had come to it about two minutes after Peter Alvares's jeep left Kundal). But I guess I must have walked more than half the distance when I had the strange encounter. I had come to a particularly thick part of the jungle, when suddenly I noticed a swaying and heaving of the bushes by the side of the road ahead of me. As I watched in fascination, a huge black bear emerged from the bushes and stepped on to the road about six metres in front of me. I immediately froze. The bear became aware of my presence only after taking two or three steps on the road. Then to my horror, turning its head towards me, it stopped and stared at me. I could not guess what intention towards me was forming in its head, but it certainly seemed to have an evil look in its eyes. For some seconds we stared at each other. Then instinctively I went into action. Yelling with all my might I raised my staff and sprang into a posture of attack. The effect was immediate. With a few bounds the bear crossed the road, and, to my great relief, disappeared into the bushes.

Now I continued on my way more warily, gripping my staff firmly, looking apprehensively to both sides of the road for any sign of movement. I longed to reach my destination. But still I had to walk for more than half an hour. At last to my joy, the road descended into the little stream. And then after walking for another ten minutes, the bright yellow cottages of Kundal came cheerfully into view.

As I cooked the evening meal I worried about my further journey into Goa. Unless Mohan arrived by next noon, I had to go down the forests of the Ghats alone. Before, my main worry had been about running into the police or their spies at Neturli, after descending from the Ghats. But now, after my encounter with the bear, I contemplated with considerable fear my solitary four-hour descent through the jungle where I imagined all sorts of dangers to be lurking. But I was determined to go the next afternoon whatever I might have to face, as I knew my long absence would frighten my home people.

I ate what I had cooked, and spread a mat and lay down, and was soon in the deep slumber of a tired young man. About midnight I was awakened by a terrible dream. All the bears from the jungles around Kundal had assembled at the door and were creating a big racket, demanding entrance into the cottage. I emerged from the dream with great fear only to realise that the cause of the dream was Mohan knocking loudly on the door and calling out: "Get up! Get up!" In a few seconds I was wide awake. Thoroughly astonished at his arrival in the middle of the night, I asked him why he had dared to walk through the jungle in the night, when he could have waited till sunrise. It was because my message passing through the medium of the tea-stall keeper of Kumbarwada had suffered a distortion. Mohan, on his arrival, had been informed that I would leave for Goa the next morning instead of the afternoon and so had directly started to walk to Kundal. When I told him of my adventure with the bear, he said, he also had been afraid of meeting with wild animals, but that he had felt emboldened with his electric torch and his stick. I wondered how he might have felt as he walked those eight miles of the fearful jungle road in the dead of the night when it is the reign of wild beasts. I really admired his courage.

His arrival made me quite happy. Now we would go down the Ghats together. And there was another reason for cheer. Mohan had brought with him a kilo of mutton which he proposed to cook immediately, for he had not had his evening meal. And unlike me he was a good cook. So about 2 o'clock in the night we had a very hearty dinner of mutton, vegetables and bread – my second meal in the night – and then with great contentment we went to sleep, getting up only late in the morning.

5

RETURN TO GOA

I had planned to leave Kundal the next afternoon, to reach Neturli at nightfall, so that we might slip into the village under cover of the dark, and then catch one of the late buses going to Sanvordem where we could spend the night. But Mohan now suggested that we spend the night out in the open, on the lower slopes of the Ghats and enter Neturli at dawn and catch any first conveyance leaving for Sanvordem. Accordingly, we thought of starting leisurely a little later in the afternoon. After our noon meal we lay down for a nap, and got up rather late. After hurried tea, we left with two small, but heavy suitcases loaded with leaflets, posters and other such material. Our descent was easier than our ascent had been, partly because we were now coming down in a different direction, where the bushes were neither so high nor so thick – we could step over most of them and proceed. But when night fell, about three hours later, we found ourselves far from Kundal – perhaps more than one third the distance still remained. Now the going became extremely difficult. We tried to see our way with the help of the electric torch, but the torch light only dazzled us and produced strange optical illusions in the surrounding greenery. So we walked on in the dark with the heavy suitcases on our shoulders, blundering through the bushes, staggering and falling, breaking our shins against hidden rocks. Our whole idea was to be as close to Neturli as possible before we rested for the night, so that with the first morning light we could enter the village. Though our progress now was very slow, still we pushed on doggedly. But after thus struggling down the slope for about an hour and a half we were so exhausted that we had hardly any strength to remain on our legs. Now there was no alternative but to spend the rest of the night where we had reached. We looked out for a leafy bush, and after beating it with a stick to drive away any snakes that might happen to be underneath; we stretched ourselves on it and slept as comfortably as the twigs of the bush poking us through our clothes allowed us.

We got up before sunrise and saw that Neturli was still about a mile away below us. Now we were anxious to reach there before it was broad daylight. But still we could not walk fast enough through the bushes, and we had yet not reached the village when the sun rose. I was then feeling quite nervous to go into the village in broad daylight, with our heavy, suspicious-looking suitcases in our hands. In fact with all this incriminating material on our hands, some nervousness remained till the end of the journey. Yet in the midst of our nervousness Mohan had the spirit to joke: "Now instead of home, we will reach police headquarters where we will be delivered to the tender care of *Agente* Monteiro and our fatigue will be well attended to."

As we were now approaching the village, we parted, to enter the village separately, and thence to travel separately by whatever conveyance each one got, up to the town of Sanvordem, where we would meet again.

Soon after separating from Mohan I saw directly ahead of me a hut which housed a restaurant; I made straight for that hut. I was happy to note that there was no one on the road to observe me. I found five or six men in the tea-house, but they were absorbed in their tea. As I sat down, only the one nearest to me looked at my suitcase and then at me. While I was drinking my tea, he again glanced at the suitcase and at me, and finally asked me where I was going. Though I was a little jittery, I answered as nonchalantly as I could that I had come to see a friend working in the mines. But the man appeared to be harmless, and I think it was only friendly inquisitiveness that had prompted him to start a conversation for which I felt the least inclination. Just then to my relief, I heard a truck coming up, and so I hurriedly got up paid for the tea and stepping on the road, put out my hand for the truck. It stopped, I got in, and was safely on my way to Sanvordem.

At the Sanvordem bus-stand I awaited Mohan's arrival with some anxiety. I had faith in his self-confidence and his resourcefulness, and I knew that with his greater experience of life he could get out of scrapes better than I could. Yet some unforeseen mishap could always occur. And there was one disadvantage under which Mohan laboured: however much he affected Goan manners and tried to speak Konkani with the Goan accent, he could not conceal his non-Goan look. In the very midst of these reflections I had the satisfaction of seeing Mohan alighting from a halted truck. As I advanced towards him through a crowd of people, he saw me, and with a look of surprise, greeted me loudly like a long-lost friend: "Hello, hello! What brings you this side?" Quite self-conscious amidst the crowd I was stammering out an answer in some confusion, when he continued, "Come, come, let's have some tea," and greatly enjoying my discomfiture he pulled me towards a restaurant.

From Sanvordem we travelled together till Margao where we parted, Mohan having reached his destination, I to continue my journey to Assonora.

My return was a great joy to my people who had been racked by great anxiety. I had promised to be back home on the third or fourth day, and here I was returning on the seventh evening. My long absence could very well have meant that I had been arrested while crossing the frontier. But I was safe home and they were happy. Seeing their joy I could not help thinking of the sorrowful day, not too distant perhaps, when I would be separated from them for months, or perhaps years. That was coming inevitably, and had to be gone through. But before that there was a lot of work to do.

6

MEMORIES OF A COMPANION IN THE STRUGGLE

During the next three months I met Mohan a number of times. He came to co-ordinate our activities with N.C.(G) activities in other parts of Goa. But never again did we share such an exciting experience as our journey to Kundal over the wild Ghats. The other meetings across the frontier that I attended were at Sanquirvale, to the north-east of Goa. And that being nearer to my place, I myself led batches of workers to those meetings. As we built up our organization in our area we began to manage our work on our own, and Mohan remained busy with his activities mostly in south Goa. And finally with my arrest I lost all contact with him.

Considering the energy and earnestness with which he had worked for the movement, I had expected him to conclude his activities by courting imprisonment, as most of the other N.C.(G) workers had done. However, it gradually dawned upon me that he had not identified himself sufficiently with the cause of Goa's freedom, as to be willing to suffer years of imprisonment for its sake. Perhaps he had loved the rigours and the risks of the struggle more than he had desired the achievement of its goal. Perhaps, he had other, more personal motives in joining the movement. However that might be, one thing was certain: though he faced risks, he had an unerring instinct for keeping himself this side of safety.

Even after my release, I had no knowledge of his whereabouts except the fact that he had evaded arrest and left Goa. But I always cherished the most fond memories of that brief but close association with him, always remembering him for his great strength, his cool courage, his adventurous spirit, and his generosity in spending what little money he had when we were together.

But though I never met him again, I very much heard of him. Some time after liberation he re-appeared in Goa and by and by established himself as a prominent trade union leader in Marmagoa. In course of time he became so powerful that he could totally paralyse the port of Marmagoa, which occasionally he did, bringing all life in the port town to a stand-still. From what I heard of him from certain friends, he seemed to have become an entirely different man from what he was in the days of the freedom struggle. He not only enjoyed his great power, but also seemed to have developed a taste for all the trappings that come with power. Even then I was in two minds whether to go and see him and renew our old friendship, until one day I saw his photograph in the newspapers. He had indeed changed beyond recognition. He looked too much the self-satisfied and self-important politician. I was sure I would not meet the young friend of those hard times in the present highly successful trade union leader. So I decided not to meet him again, preferring to keep alive the memory of that dear true friend, so generous and so courageous, rather than allowing it to die in that strange labour leader. I have realised that sometimes it is wiser not to meet some persons twice in one's life-time: they turn out to be so disappointing on renewed acquaintance.

7

WE ESTABLISH A NETWORK OF PATRIOTIC CELLS

After my return from Kundal, we began the work of the freedom movement in earnest. We already had a group of five patriots in Aldona to start with, the group which together with myself formed the initial nucleus of our organization in this area. We all assembled together at Aldona the next evening, and I presented a report of the meeting at Kundal. We then decided as a first step to enlarge our cell in Aldona and also to set up a cell in Assonora. In both these places we knew people who would be sympathetic to the cause of the freedom struggle, and some who would also be willing to work actively for the cause.

Among the initial group in Aldona were three of our teachers – respected, well-informed, middle-aged people. The rest were my school companions. The teachers being men with serious family responsibilities, could not be expected to be so very active, but they helped us with their very valuable guidance. And most of all their maturity and good sense lent a high seriousness and a kind of moral authority to our activities which otherwise might sometimes have appeared to us as merely an expression of our juvenile enthusiasm.

Soon we had strong cells of reliable workers at Aldona and at Assonora. But we did not wish to confine our work to these two villages alone. We knew that though our organization, the N.C.(G), was well-established in the nearby towns of Mapusa and Bicholim, in many of the neighbouring villages our movement had not reached at all. We decided to try to extend our organization to some of these villages. Our usual procedure was to approach only those people who were well-known to us, and who, we thought, could be trusted, and very cautiously to sound them on their attitude to the freedom movement. Many times we drew blanks. Some persons showed themselves to be indifferent to the movement, some to be downright hostile, and then we ourselves had to feign indifference. Some showed great interest in the movement but when it was proposed to them that we ourselves should work for it they shrank back in fear. Only a few were bold enough to offer to work for the freedom of Goa in whatever way they could, and to these we revealed that we were already members of N.C.(G), and we got them enrolled in their turn.

Thus in the course of about two months we succeeded in establishing small additional cells in the villages of Chorão, Tivim and Siolim. It was a matter of some satisfaction to us that within such a short time, and starting from scratch, we had built up such a widespread revolutionary organization. Still we were far from our final goal of a mass struggle. I was dreaming of the time, when we would be able to hold open, public meetings to demand freedom for Goa, in each of the villages where we had our organization. I chafed under the restraints of caution and secrecy that we had to work with, for even at that time I realised that a non-violent movement finally had to be an open movement, and that secrecy after a certain point defeated the very purpose of a non-violent struggle. But for the time being we had to work in secrecy, because at this stage we could not expect the Goan people to support the freedom movement to the extent of attending public nationalist meetings. It was not that most of the people were unpatriotic. There were many people who were patriotic in their own way, and there was a lot of sympathy for the movement. But it was a lukewarm sympathy, their patriotism was a pusillanimous sort of patriotism. In trying to mobilise mass support for the movement we had to fight people's apathy and their fear.

The post-liberation generation who are now accustomed to seeing people combine for a collective purpose will find it difficult to imagine the degree of apathy that prevailed at that time. People in those days just could not conceive the notion that some undesirable situation could be changed by collective action. They passively accepted whatever authority imposed upon them. This apathy was the result of four and a half centuries of colonial rule which had killed all collective initiative in the people. And linked with their apathy was their fear. Fear of the government, fear of the police particularly, fear of incurring the wrath of anyone in authority. And there was also in many people a fear of the white man regarded as a superior being, destined to rule. It could be no exaggeration to say that it was a veritable reign of fear in those days. If a neighbour was arrested for nationalist activities, people would shun the neighbour's household and talk about the arrest in hushed whispers in the privacy of their homes. Those who were suspected to be in the freedom movement were avoided like the plague.

There were many bold spirits, however, who shook off the prevailing apathy and fear and joined the freedom movement, and in course of time there was an increasing number of such people who were prepared to face arrest for their convictions. But we could not throw off the colonial yoke unless our movement became a mass struggle, and for that we needed the support of the Goan people in general. But how to get the people out of the clutches of apathy and fear so that they openly supported the freedom movement? How to inspire the people with faith in their own collective strength? It was a stupendous task. We did not know whether we were equal to that task but we had to try our utmost. By various means we had to keep the struggle constantly before the attention of the people. We found that one of the effective means of agitating the minds of the people was the display of our propaganda material -- flags, posters, leaflets and pamphlets. A large-scale use of this material made a very great impact on the minds of people.

We would go about late in the night, usually two together on a bicycle, carrying a bundle of the material. And we would paste posters and flags on compound walls, trees, telegraph poles and on mile-stones all along the roads; and in the bazars and market-places we would scatter leaflets and pamphlets. We would have great amusement thinking of the consternation that would be caused by the sudden appearance of these shocking things to the local police and the village *regedores* (headmen) whose business it would be to remove these things from public view. In the morning, before these petty authorities became aware of them, they were seen and read by many people. They created a great sensation. People were made to realise that the freedom movement had reached right in their villages. They began to talk about it, albeit privately and in whispers.

The propaganda material could not be displayed everyday, as it would be easier for the police to lie in wait for us and surprise us in the very act of scattering it. It was decided to use it three or four times in the month and each village cell was left free to choose their own days. But there were certain occasions of special significance, like Indian national days, when we displayed this material in every village at the same time. I remember in particular Republic Day, January 26, 1955 when we displayed it on a very lavish scale together in all the villages in which we had our cells. Its impact had been tremendous. Everyone was now feeling that the movement was assuming serious proportions and the government on their part intensified police patrolling from that day.

The work of displaying the propaganda material was rather a risky business. It had to be done first of all without arousing the suspicion of the petty local government functionaries. Of course, as the work was done at night, there was nothing to fear from the *regedor* and the local police spies who would be fast asleep when we were up and active. The police spies no doubt could report us if they suspected us; and had they gone about their business a little more shrewdly, they certainly could have smelt our activities. But the spies of those days were a stupid lot; they were usually recruited from the dregs of society, from among idlers, hooligans and social misfits. It was quite easy to detect them: they betrayed themselves by their boasting and swaggering; it was not unusual to come upon one of them drinking in a bar or tavern and boasting of his new job and of his power to send his enemies behind bars. We only had to keep a low profile before them, and we were safe from them. The local police constables also did not bother us much as at night they mostly remained confined to their police posts.

Our main worry when we went out with the propaganda material was the police patrols coming from the Mapusa and Bicholim police stations and sometimes from Panjim police headquarters. These police parties consisting of five to eight men, most of them white men, would come at any time in the night by jeep, or van, or car, or sometimes even by motorcycles. They would be well-armed, each party carrying one or two stenguns, besides other weapons. We had to avoid them by all means. Even if we had managed to throw away the incriminating material in time, two young fellows found going by cycle late in the night, in those days of the movement, would be suspect in their eyes, and we would be sure to be hauled to the police station without further ado. What helped us was that in those days there was very little traffic at night, and the roads would be quiet and dark (there being no electricity except in major towns); so that the occasional vehicle that came up once in about half an hour could be heard and its headlights could be seen from a distance of about two kilometres. We had to suppose that every motor vehicle that approached could be a police vehicle. And while going about our work we had to keep a sharp look-out. As soon as we heard the sound of a vehicle or saw its headlights, we would take our cycle into a side-road or where that was not available, we would look for some roadside bushes and would go and crouch behind them till the vehicle passed. Every time, that we, from the Assonora cell went out for this work, we were interrupted three or four times at least by the approach of some vehicle, for it was a long stretch of road we had to cover, right from Assonora bazar till about the borders of Mapusa, a distance of more than ten kilometres. And inspite of all the precautions we took we did face risks sometimes.

Once, we had a narrow escape. Two of us were on our way home and had reached Tivim, when all at once I, sitting on the hind carrier of the bicycle saw behind us the beams of a vehicle's headlights piercing the dark night-sky, as the vehicle came up a slope. We stopped. There was neither a side road nor a bush nearby. We could only go into the roadside ditch. We hurriedly found a deeper part of the ditch, and having lowered the cycle into it, we also jumped in, one after the other, and lay flat at the bottom. Soon we saw the vehicle's light brightening up the ground above us leaving the ditch in darkness. But just a moment after it passed above us, to our great dismay, with a terrific screech it halted only about thirty metres away from us. We wondered whether they had caught a glimpse of us, and were coming to us. We heard car doors opening and men coming out and talking and cursing in Portuguese. It was a police patrol! We waited with trepidation for some moments, but no one came towards us. Only then, did we cautiously raise our heads and see a Land Rover halted at the foot of a tree, and three men looking at a sheet of paper in the headlights of the vehicle. We now understood what had stopped them. It was one of our large posters pasted on a tree-trunk. As we lay huddled in the ditch, we still feared that they might make a search around. But they had no reason for suspecting that the culprits responsible for the posters were so near, and soon after they got into their vehicle and drove off.

Besides using the propaganda material, we tried other methods of agitation. As time went on we began to feel that the great secrecy in which we carried on our activities would not allow us to make much headway, and we began to adopt bolder methods to get more and more people into the movement. Our workers in each village would make a list of youngsters in their respective villages, youngsters who were not likely to be prejudiced towards the freedom struggle. Then our workers pretending to be complete strangers to the movement would go and inform the youngsters of a certain meeting of the freedom fighters scheduled for that night in a lonely part of the village. Then a group of four or five of us not known in that particular village would go and address the meeting. There was some risk in holding such pre-announced meetings. But we took the precaution of posting some of our workers at the approach ways to watch whether any dangerous elements were coming towards the venue of the meeting. These meetings were not big affairs – we never had more than eight youngsters attending – but at that time we were satisfied with that little progress in our work. Most of the youngsters who came offered to help the movement in some way or the other; they were at least prepared to display the propaganda material which we supplied to them. We also invited some of them to come with us to meet the N.C. (G) leaders across the frontier, which a few of them did. These village-level meetings did help us in expanding our organisation.

In the course of our work of expanding the organisation, we had sometimes the experience of coming across aggressive youngsters who urged that we employ violent methods in our struggle. They proposed that we should blow up bridges and government buildings and shoot at police patrols, and they even offered to procure the necessary explosives and firearms. It was not very difficult to obtain explosives in those days as many mine workers who had access to magazines in their mines used to bring them out surreptitiously and use them for killing fish in rivers and ponds, and sometimes even sell them secretly. As to firearms, many people in those times possessed unlicensed muzzle-loading guns, some of them country made. It was with some difficulty that we restrained these youngsters with violent tendencies; but we made it clear to them that our N.C (G) organisation was strictly committed to non-violence and that we would not want anyone associated with our organisation to indulge in any act of violence.

8

MORE MEETINGS ACROSS THE BORDER

Early in January of 1955 we received word that the next meeting across the border, for workers of North Goa was going to be held soon at Sanquirvale. Though there were no great decisions to be taken at these meetings nor were there important new instructions to be given to the workers (the actual *modus operandi* of the work inside Goa being left to the workers themselves), still for a number of reasons we made it a point to attend these meetings. For one thing, we obtained a complete picture of the progress of the movement in Goa from the reports that workers from various parts of Goa presented about developments in their respective areas. We learnt from these reports, for instance, that all the time there were arrests, here and there in Goa, of people suspected of nationalist activities; there was otherwise no means of knowing about these arrests, as the Goan censored press did not report them, nor did the people talk much about them. Another reason for our attending the meetings was that we wanted as many of our new workers as possible to have the experience of crossing the frontier and meeting our leader Peter Alvares so that they might be inspired with enthusiasm for the work of the movement. By this time Peter Alvares had gained legendary fame among Goans as the man who launched the non-violent movement against Portuguese rule in August, 1954, and many of our workers eagerly seized the opportunity to meet the man and take directions from him. And though he gave no new directions but only exhorted us to intensify the struggle in Goa, so that the next phase of the movement with people from all over India participating could begin early, our workers were quite impressed, and returned from these meetings to work with greater zeal. Yet another attraction of these meetings was that for us youngsters they implied the thrill of undertaking a risky journey by night, the great adventure of illegally crossing the border, evading the Portuguese frontier patrols. And finally, it was necessary for some of us to go and bring periodically the propaganda material from across the border, and we combined this necessity with the occasion of the meeting.

Beginning with the January meeting we attended altogether three meetings at Sanquirvale, and everytime it was I who took the responsibility of leading there a batch of our workers. Sanquirvale is about 10 kilometres from my village Assonora. I had travelled there by road some years before, but now we had to go walking in the dark, finding our way through forests and over hills, because going along the Assonora-Sanquirvale road even under cover of the dark was unthinkable – this road, being one that led to the frontier was heavily patrolled. Though I only knew the direction in which Sanquirvale lay, I felt I would be equal to the task of leading our companions through the wild, difficult terrain.

There were nine of us who attended the January meeting. Our companions coming from Aldona, Chorão, Tivim and Siolim all assembled at Assonora in the evening, and after night-fall we set out, striking in a north-easterly direction. Upon leaving the village we were at once in the safety of the hills. In fact it would be possible to go safely through the hills and forests the whole way from Assonora to the Sanquirvale border without coming upon any human habitation provided one were thoroughly familiar with the terrain, and could follow a route skirting the small forest villages that lie along the way – primitive villages like those of Advalpale, Uspa and Cansarpale. Some of these villages are tucked in hills and forests, and in those days particularly, these simple, primitive hamlets with their little mud houses were so much a part of their natural surroundings and were so well concealed in them that even in the day time it was quite difficult to locate them, and at night quite impossible. I led our party safely past the first neighbouring village, Advalpale, as I was familiar with its surrounding. But as we advanced further it became difficult to make out in the dark night what lay ahead of us even at a distance of about a hundred metres, and before we were aware of it we blundered right into a village, rousing all the dogs in it and setting them barking furiously at us, which in turn woke the villagers, some of whom stole out of their houses into the cold night wrapped in black blankets (kambals) to peer in the star light at the strange procession passing through their village. For a few moments I was afraid that they might call out in alarm. But they only followed us silently for some time, as we hurriedly tried to get clear of their village. It was a queer sensation indeed seeing those dark, indistinct figures gliding noiselessly like ghosts among the tree trunks behind us. And it was quite a relief when we extricated ourselves from the village and emerged on some open ground, and they ceased to follow us. They must have been trying to make out what we were. Perhaps they had finally decided that we were a party of smugglers.

As we proceeded through forests and over hills, we had frequently to determine our bearings. When we happened to be on high, open ground, we could find our direction by certain distant mountains to the east, whose positions and shapes I was familiar with, and which could be seen now in faint outline. But when we were walking in forests or on hill-slopes and those mountains were hidden from view, then my little knowledge of the stars proved very useful. Now and then I scanned the sky for the Pole Star or for Orion and Sirius, and then solemnly pointed out our direction, all the while feeling myself quite a wizard for having this knowledge, and enjoying the admiration with which my companions regarded me.

Though we were confident that we were going in the right direction, there was no way of knowing how far we were from Sanquirvale. The place was without electric lights in those days. I knew that it was situated a few furlongs from the Goa frontier. I had also been informed that on the Goan side a road ran parallel to the frontier, quite close to it. This frontier road was heavily patrolled by the Portuguese police, and that was our worry.

About 11 o'clock, we had come upon quite open, level ground dotted with clumps of bushes here and there. By then I had a feeling that we were close to the frontier and to Sanquirvale. But the whole land before us lay quiet and dark, and peer as we would into the gloom, we could not make out any distinct features in the terrain except for the nearest clumps of bushes. All the same I now thought of taking certain precautions. I cautioned my companions not to speak save in whispers, and to tread as softly as possible. I also thought of taking cover of the clumps of bushes, and led them from one clump to another, though this meant frequently changing directions. While we were thus carefully proceeding, there appeared to the south of us headlights of a vehicle. It moved slowly in the northern direction, a few furlongs in front of us, towards the village of Sal. Undoubtedly it was a police patrol vehicle, and its passage had marked for us the position of the frontier road.

I could sense now the mounting tension that gripped everyone of us. We were about to enter the danger zone. The danger lay not so much in the passing patrol vehicles, but in police parties on foot (as we had been informed) sometimes stationed at certain points to watch the frontier road by night. We had to proceed now with the utmost care. I instructed our companions to crouch and walk still more stealthily, and I got all those who wore white or bright-coloured shirts to remove them. Thus we advanced, stopping frequently to listen, and when we judged that we had come within a furlong of the road, we waited and listened for about fifteen minutes. The profound silence that prevailed did not seem to reassure us, but on the contrary seemed to hold a greater threat of danger. There were fewer clumps of bushes now, but, we thought, any one of them might conceal a police party. And before us seemed to stretch the same impenetrable gloom with no visible sign of the road, though we knew it was near. At last we decided to move and cross at one stretch the road and then the frontier. I rose and led the way, the others following in single file, crouching so low that they seemed to be going on all fours. After a minute we suddenly came to the road. It had not been visible because it was almost level with the ground. And then after walking for another minute, we knew we were safely across the frontier.

On our return journey we crossed the frontier on the advice of some local people, at a point further to the north, and we did it with greater confidence though with the usual caution. Our fear on the first crossing might have been mainly due to this frontier being totally new to us, and as we familiarised ourselves with those border areas, we could in fact cross it with greater and greater ease, in our subsequent trips to Sanquirvale. But I always tried to bear in mind the risk we courted. This sector of the frontier being more accessible and hence comparatively more convenient to cross, was consequently more effectively guarded by Portuguese police. Every time that I led a batch to Sanquirvale, I was careful about taking certain precautions like walking with great stealth and taking cover of bushes as we approached the frontier road, and finally halting and listening for some time before crossing the frontier. That these precautions were necessary was brought home to us at the time of returning from our third meeting at Sanquirvale.

9

A BRUSH WITH A POLICE PARTY

I led a batch of seven workers for our third meeting at Sanquirvale some time in February, 1955. After the meeting we left Sanquirvale on our homeward journey, about midnight, all laden with rather heavy bags of propaganda material. Each one of us had, as usual, armed himself with a stout stick which could be used for support while walking through brushwood or on the highly uneven ground. But now most of us had hung the bags on the sticks and slung them behind our shoulders, the sticks resting on the shoulders musket fashion. On approaching the frontier we had as usual stopped and listened for any unusual sound, and then we had crossed both the frontier and the road without any mishap. After having covered a distance of about a furlong from the road we were feeling quite safe, and were walking along, in a relaxed manner, spread out in a little arc. A half moon had come up behind us, but the sky in the east being cloudy, there was no clear, bright moonlight. We were now on open ground which gently sloped down westwards, and in the dim moonlight we could discern not only the clumps of bushes scattered on the open ground, but also a stretch of forest at the bottom of the slope about a hundred metres away. We were passing a clump of bushes to the south of us when I, walking at the northern end of the arc suddenly noticed with utter astonishment, two of our fellows at the other end bolting away. As I looked in that direction trying to understand the cause of their fright, I saw three or four human figures with the unmistakable police caps on their heads rising up from the bushes about ten metres away from us. By then our other companions saw them, and two more bolted, all four rushing for the shelter of the forest. The rest, though startled walked with me at the same pace. I was thinking it was unwise to run, as it might tempt the police to open fire, and I was all the time expecting to be challenged, or worse still, to hear shots. But nothing happened, and soon we were behind another clump of bushes which provided some cover. We could now hear our four runners crashing through the forest, and we ourselves had to run through the thorny undergrowth of the forest to overtake them. When we finally caught up with them I asked everyone to sit quietly, and we held a little council.

I felt that the danger was not all past. It was a great mystery to us why they had made no attempt to intercept us. Perhaps we had come too suddenly upon them and they had no time to react. In that case, by now having had time to collect their wits, they might decide to follow us and to waylay us as we emerged from the forest, which as we had observed from the top of the slope, was not quite extensive. And if they were intent on following us, they might have traced our progress through the forest by listening to the terrific noise we made while crashing through it, and now they might even have roughly located our position. These were our anxious thoughts as we huddled under the trees.

And to add to our troubles one of our companions began to complain of pain in his ankle. He had sprained his leg while running recklessly in the forest. He examined it feeling it with his hands in the dark, and found it already swollen.

The first thing we decided on was to move noiselessly to the edge of the forest and see what prospect we faced. We helped the fellow who had sprained his leg to get on his feet. He found walking quite painful, but with his arms on the shoulders of two companions, one on each side, he managed to limp along. Our homeward direction was south-west, but we found the forest elongated more westwards; so we thought of going westward in order to take more advantage of the shelter provided by the forest, and to put greater distance between us and the police party. We advanced with the utmost caution possible, so that we might not betray our position to them, in case they were listening outside the forest.

When we reached the edge, I thought it was best to wait there a long time and watch and listen. If they were watching from somewhere near, I thought we could wear them with our patience: if we remained quiet for long enough, they might believe we had given them the slip, and they might give up their watch and reveal themselves by some sound or movement. We quietly sat and waited. In our state of heightened anxiety, we were sometimes alarmed by certain sounds around us. But they turned out to be the normal sounds of the forest, like small animals treading on dry leaves, or night fowls stirring in the foliage of trees.

After half an hour we thought of venturing forth. There was brighter moonlight now, but the prospect before us was not so bad: not only was the ground dotted with the usual clumps of bushes, but there were some big trees here and there in whose dark shades we could walk unseen. Everyone was tense with fear as we left the shelter of the forest and advanced, crouching, keeping ourselves in the darkness provided by bushes and trees. Our poor cripple had to walk unaided for some time, as it was impossible for others to support him and walk crouching at the same time. But he understood the demand of the situation and bravely hobbled along, bearing all the pain. As we covered a couple of furlongs we gradually relaxed with a sense of relief, feeling that the danger was past. We were glad to escape from the police party with no harm to ourselves than an ankle sprain suffered by one, and cuts and scratches all over the body, specially the legs, sustained by all as a result of running through the bushes and briars in the forest. Our cripple had to be supported all the way to Assonora, a distance of not less than eight miles through difficult terrain; but as most of our companions were exhausted with the exertions and excitement of the escape, and hardly had strength to trudge through the weary miles, the work of supporting the invalid fell mainly on me, as the leader of our group. By the time we staggered into Assonora a little before dawn, the invalid's leg was badly swollen; and he had to remain resting at my house and be treated with some home remedies. Only late in the evening could I carry him on my bicycle to his house in Siolim. [This freedom fighter, Gurudas Naik of Siolim was one of our enthusiastic workers; but he was not in prison with us. As soon as some of us were arrested he went underground and helped the movement all along.] As for others, the only after effect we suffered was that the daily bath, with the myriad of scratches on the body, proved to be a veritable torture for a number of days.

We could never fully explain to ourselves the mystery why that police party behaved in the way they did, making no effort to apprehend us. That it was a police party, there was no doubt in our minds. Most of us, including myself had clearly seen their tell-tale caps and their khaki tunics. Some who had walked nearest to them even claimed to have seen the glint of moonlight on their rifles. A likely explanation is that the entire party consisted of Goan personnel who had not wished to take unnecessary risks for the benefit of their Portuguese masters. They might have been unnerved by the sudden appearance of a large number of people before them. Perhaps in the dim moonlight they had mistaken the sticks that we carried on our shoulders for guns, and had not wished to take any chance with a supposedly armed group. According to the information we had collected about the movements of the police in the border areas, the European personnel whether hailing from Bicholim and Mapusa police stations, or from Panjim headquarters usually patrolled the frontier road in motor vehicles. It was Goan personnel from the Bicholim station that were sometimes transported in vans and dropped in small groups at certain points on the frontier road and left to guard the frontier at night. We could well imagine such a group of disgruntled Goan policemen left to shiver, out in the cold night, carrying out their duty half-heartedly.

That was our only brush with the police while crossing the frontier. And as it happened that was the last time we crossed the border to attend a meeting. Later I always remembered those meetings across the frontier with great nostalgia, and regretted that I could not attend more of them; for the adventure of those night journeys out in the wild, under the glimmer of the starry skies, with the final fear and thrill of crossing a guarded frontier appealed to something deep down in one's nature. The next meeting at Sanquirvale was scheduled for the third week of March, and I was preparing to attend it with another batch of workers, when the great eventuality, always feared to be round the corner came about and prevented us from attending it.

10

MY ARREST

By the beginning of March, 1955 we had quite a well-knit organization in the areas we were operating in, with its twin coordinating centres, Assonora and Aldona where the workers from the outlying villages used to contact us and receive instructions. Our main work continued to be the display of the propoganda material, which we now used on a larger scale, having a larger and quicker supply of the same through Sanquirvale. We could feel that the display of this material was having its impact; it was mainly through its display that the freedom struggle was made to impinge upon the consciousness of our people, particularly uneducated Goans. Besides using propaganda material, we tried to influence people individually through discreet personal contacts, while taking care not to meet people known for their pro-Portuguese sympathies. The result of all this work done by us was that there was a noticeable change in people's attitude to the freedom struggle. Many people were now for the first time contemplating the end of Portuguese rule, some even thinking it to be quite near. There were also many who knew of our involvement in the movement, and yet looked upon it with some approval, or at least did not do anything to betray us.

But still we were very far from our goal of a mass struggle. What we envisaged by a mass struggle was that there would be large scale risings and demonstrations in all villages and towns of Goa which would make it impossible for the Portuguese to continue ruling Goa. We were inexperienced idealists in those days, and in our naivete we supposed that in about a year, our N.C.(G) would be able to mobilise the Goan people to the extent of getting them out on the streets in large masses demanding an end to Portuguese rule, and being ready to face police brutalities and imprisonment. By contrast, what had been achieved so far all over Goa was the establishment of the N.C.(G) units in practically every town and village, and as a result of the efforts of all these units, some change in the attitudes of people. People were more sympathetic to the movement, but very few were prepared to make the great sacrifice of courting arrest and going to jail. Our consolation lay in the fact that it was not a stagnant situation. On the contrary it was indeed very dynamic. The movement was very much alive with hundreds of patriots being active in the work of propaganda and agitation; and it was slowly growing with more people being gradually drawn into the movement. Arrests were continuing all over Goa, most of those arrested being N.C.(G) workers. Also, now and then, on certain significant occasions, some of the N.C.(G) workers in small groups offered *Satyagraha* in the main towns of Goa.

All the same it was painfully slow work getting the people actively involved in the freedom struggle, and some of us eager idealists, impatient for quick results, chafed under the slow tempo of the movement. The usual work with which we had occupied ourselves for months now began to appear rather ineffective, and dull and stale. The arrests of fellow patriots also deeply affected us and increased our restlessness. We had known some of them, having met them at the meetings across the frontier, and being together engaged in the work of the great cause, we had forged emotional ties of comradeship with them. And they by going to jail, had risen in our estimation as patriots beyond all reproach. For by being arrested or by offering *satyagraha*, they had made by their very person, their great final contribution to the cause. We were now assailed by doubts whether the continuation of our work outside served any great purpose, or whether we could serve the cause better by ourselves going to prison.

No doubt, it was an idea tacitly agreed upon by all, that our activities in this non-violent movement were to culminate in our holding a public demonstration and courting arrest. We were well aware of the fact that the strength of a non-violent movement derives mainly from people's willingness to go to prison. But the only question was of timing – was the time ripe for us to wind up our work outside and go to jail? When I broached this subject of our courting imprisonment with many of our companions, particularly those who had been working with me from the beginning, some of them demurred and pleaded for time. They argued that we could still do useful work remaining out of jail. I could understand their hesitation.

It was not easy to decide to go to prison. It had not been easy for me too. Opposing the Portuguese regime and courting arrest implied not merely the readiness to undergo the rigors of prison life for an indefinite period, but also the willingness to face the brutalities of the notorious Portuguese police.

By the middle of March the question of when to court imprisonment was left undecided. The 6th of April, the date commemorating the Jalianwala Bagh victims, was fast approaching and some patriots from other parts of Goa were to offer *satyagraha* in some of the towns. After that would come the 18th of June, the date on which Lohia initiated the 1946 movement, when more patriots would have to volunteer for *satyagraha*, and I hoped our group would be ready by then. I thought it was worth giving our companions enough time to prepare themselves, provided, we could get together a large group (I was expecting about 25 people), and hold a big impressive demonstration which would really jolt the people of our area out of their political lethargy.

We made our plans, but fate disposed of things in her own way. We used to take normal precautions in our work to escape the notice of certain police spies stationed in villages. But a non-violent movement, by its very nature cannot be conducted in too much secrecy. We were ever prepared for the possibility of our whole group being exposed by someone reporting any one of our workers to the police. But finally we were betrayed by a treacherous friend of one of our workers from Siolim. That traitor, perhaps to gain some favour from some petty government authority, ferreted out information about our group from our worker, and then passed it on to a police spy.

On the 19th of March we thought of displaying the propaganda material. About 9 o'clock in the night a companion from Assonora and I started on our bicycle and rode up the Assonora-Mapusa road scattering leaflets and pasting posters all the way. We completed our work and began to return without having experienced anything unusual save that three or four times we had to go into hiding when different motor vehicles came up, one of them a van which we had suspected to be a police vehicle. About 11.30 we left the main road and turned into the lane leading to my house. After the tension and fatigue of the work, we were glad to be on our way home, and were thinking of the food and bed that awaited us. I was riding the cycle carrying my companion on the front bar. My friend was now using an electric torch to light up the rough, uneven mud road. As we approached our house the torch beam suddenly picked up a figure dressed in a white banyan and khaki shorts. He was standing under a mango tree about thirty-five metres away from us, but when the torch light fell on him, he slowly and deliberately began to advance towards us. He was not a white man, but we could make out he was a policeman. My companion, Rafael, called on me in a hoarse whisper to stop. My first impulse like my companion's was to throw the cycle and bolt. But I did some quick thinking. Most probably the man was not alone, there might be more men hiding behind the tree trunk or behind the stone wall which bordered one side of the road. Running away involved the risk of being shot in the back (even ordinary Portuguese constables carried revolvers); and if there were three or four men shooting, we could hardly expect them all to miss their targets. And even if we succeeded in escaping, our home people were sure to be harassed by the police. And finally, I thought, we had to face this situation sooner or later: we had to fall into the hands of the police to reach our destination – jail; then why not now? So, saying to my companion, "Let's see what happens," I slowed the cycle, but went on. My companion still kept the torch beam on the man, who we could see now, was advancing all prepared for action. When we reached him he seized the steering bar of the cycle with both hands and with all his might tried to stop us. I dismounted and my companion also jumped down, but the momentum of the cycle carried all three of us a few metres with a prodigious tramping of feet. In the same instant four men jumped onto the road from across the wall and flung themselves at us, nearly knocking us over, one of them, who appeared to be in command, shouting *Calma! Calma!* These four, all white men, pinned down our hands, and the man in command, a police *Agente* (detective) hurriedly felt us all over to see if we carried any weapons. Thereupon, I took the opportunity of telling him that we had no weapons, as we belonged to the non-violent movement and that we would willingly go with them. That seemed to please him. *Esta bem*, he said. "Leave their hands," he ordered his men. We saw that two of the men carried stenguns, and they walked one by our side and the other behind us.

Thus escorted we reached our house. I had never felt reluctant to return to the dear little home as I felt then, being in the custody of the police. When I saw light coming from the open front door, I knew that my mother and sister were sitting in the verandah awaiting our return. They must already have heard the heavy tramping of jack-boots outside, for before we entered they were standing frozen with fear, and staring in the dim light at the khaki-clad figures entering the house. In a few seconds they must have taken in the situation. To put them at their ease I called out to my sister, in as even a voice as I could manage and said, "We have to go with these gentlemen." The officer in charge, then greeted the ladies and said he wanted to search the house. They went through our bookracks, trunks, and clothes drawers, the officer directing his men to put back in their places the things they turned up. The search yielded them nothing more than some of our propaganda material, which they seized. When we were on the point of leaving, my sister asked the officer whether he would permit us to eat our food before we left. "They have not had their food ?" he said, "of course they can eat." And they patiently waited around us while my companion and I along with my mother and sister tried to eat the food for which, in those circumstances, we had little relish.

After our meal, I went up with a heavy heart to my mother and my sister to bid them farewell. As I embraced her, my mother broke down and began to sob, while I vainly tried to comfort her, telling her that we would meet very soon. The officer then laid his hand upon her shoulder, and said in a kind voice, *Vai voltar logo* – He is going to return soon. He was indeed a decent man. This is the first person from the 'enemy' camp that I always remember with gratitude – for having behaved like a gentleman in our house and specially for those few consoling words to my mother – *Vai voltar logo.*[1]

In the meantime one of the men had been sent by the officer to bring up the van which they had concealed far from our house, and which now came up. It was the same van which we had passed on the main road and suspected to be a police vehicle.

As the van started to move I cast a last lingering look at the dear old house, and the two sad figures standing in the verandah. I wondered when I would see again the dear place which had been the scene of all the memories of my childhood and boyhood; and the two loved ones who had been so much a part of my life and from whom I

---

1. [The name of this officer who arrested us, we learnt later, was Santos-Junior. The Goan policeman with them was a corporal named Sukdo.]

was now being wrenched away. But I had no illusions. I knew it would be a long separation. I knew that once the portal of prison closed on me, it would not open again, for years perhaps. What was particularly painful at the time of that separation was the contemplation that I was leaving behind two helpless women to a life of loneliness and sorrow.

11

IN MAPUSA POLICE CUSTODY

I Taste Prison and Face the First Police Interrogator

The police party which had arrested us had come from Mapusa police station, where they now took us, and shut us up in a small, bare room with a grill door, but no windows. We surmised that this room served as a provisional custody-room and that we were likely to be transferred soon to a more permanent prison-cell. But it was past midnight now, and most of the police personnel including those who had arrested us must have retired for the night, and so we thought, we would have to spend the rest of the night in that room without being able to sleep, unless we were prepared to lie on the bare dusty floor. However, we had no desire for sleep. The thought of the ordeal of our interrogation we had to go through, took complete possession of our minds. We wondered in what manner it would be conducted, what sorts of methods they would use against us. It would be difficult to describe the anxiety and fear that gripped our minds all that night as we waited for the morning to dawn, and for the interrogation to begin. Our throats were painfully parched with that anxiety and fear, and all the time we felt a great need of water. There was an elderly constable, a Goan, on sentry duty near our room. We called to him and requested him to give us some drinking water. He went and brought it in two plastic tumblers. After twenty minutes our throats were painfully dry again, and we asked for more water. Again he patiently went and brought two tumblerfulls. When after about another twenty minutes we asked for water the third time, he remarked with apparent annoyance, "How much water you fellows drink!" and went and disappeared for five minutes.

We thought he did not further want to oblige us. But finally the good man reappeared with a pot full of water, enough to last us till the morning. In the kind of circumstances in which we found ourselves, we were much moved by that little act of kindness; and in the course of our long imprisonment there were a number of such kind acts done to us by strangers and by men who were taught to consider us as enemies.

We spent the rest of the night sitting on the floor and talking – preparing ourselves for the forthcoming interrogation. One of the things that particularly worried me was how my companion Rafael would fare in the interrogation: I was afraid that he might contradict himself in his statements, or that they might not tally with mine. In that case the interrogating officer would only be too glad to use violent methods against us. I considered it a good fortune that we were not separated immediately on being brought in, and I made good use of the time trying to coach my companion for the interrogation. I made him follow a simple strategy. He was to say that his activities were confined to our village, and were all carried out under my direction; as to other things like our meetings across the border, or the identity of the other members of our group, he was to feign complete ignorance. But about his work in the village, he should give a wholly truthful account. In fact, this strategy proved to be quite effective in his case.

Early in the morning we were taken out to answer nature's call, and then separated. I was put in a cell already occupied by a boy of fifteen, and my companion was put in the adjacent cell. The boy, Atul, had been arrested, a month before, for possessing some nationalist posters. He was a plucky little fellow with an irrepressible spirit which nothing could dampen. He was happy to have my company, and at once began to ply me with questions about the reason of my arrest, about my work in the movement – questions which, in my state of anxiety, I was little inclined to answer to his satisfaction.

I was thinking I might be taken for questioning at any time now. Some time after we were given tea and bread, I heard my companion Rafael's name being called out, and then the door of the adjacent cell being thrown open. I had been expecting myself to be taken first for questioning; but perhaps by chance, perhaps by design, they had taken Rafael first. I was then on pins and needles, listening at the door, awaiting Rafael's return. After about an hour I heard the sound of approaching footsteps in the corridor outside, and then the door of the next cell being opened and closed. I thought my turn would come immediately. But minutes passed and no one came for me.

"If only, I could have a word with Rafael" I thought aloud. "You want to speak to him?" Atul said, "Wait." He had already established a secret channel of communication with the next cell. He first went to the door and listened through the grill-opening to find whether the sentry was moving about in the corridor; then he stepped back and with a piece of tile he struck a few times on the wall separating the two cells. Soon there were answering taps from the other side of the wall. At once he went back to the door and softly calling a certain prisoner who had come to the door of the other cell, said to him, "Call Rafael to the door."

"Rafael" I called, "How was it?" "It was all right," he said, "I stuck to the story you gave me, and there was no trouble. But they seem to have all the information."

"Listen," I called out, "I don't think we will be brought together again. But if they take you out for further questioning, stick to the same story, whatever pressure they put upon you."

It was only after half an hour that I was taken to the room of the Station Commandant, *Tenente* (lieutenant) Ribeiro, who himself conducted the interrogation. As I was ushered into his room in one glance I tried to judge his nature. My impression was that he was a stern man, but rather too dignified to be brutal. With due courtesy I wished him good day. Without answering the greeting he asked: *Fala Portugues?* – Do you speak Portuguese? I replied that I knew a little Portuguese. "Will you be able to answer my questions in Portuguese?" I said I thought I would be able to.

I was nervous, no doubt, but quite determined at the same time not to cringe before any of the investigating officers. I fortified my courage with the thought that ours was a just cause, that though the Portuguese government had the power to arrest us, prosecute us and condemn us, their position here in Goa was nothing better than that of oppressors and bullies; whereas we had the honour of being patriots serving the noble cause of freedom. It was this thought that enabled me to face the police interrogators with a sense of moral superiority.

There was a police corporal, a Goan, sitting at a typewriter, who served as *tenente* Ribeiro's secretary, and when occasion required, as interpreter. The Commandant left me standing and began questioning me and dictating my statement to the secretary. After taking my name and other personal particulars, he asked me whether I belonged to any subversive organisation working against Portuguese Sovereignty. I replied that I was a member of National Congress (Goa), a patriotic organisation of Goans: "And what was its aim?" he asked. "To free Goa from Portuguese rule," I answered.

At that he glared and growled at me for some time, but finally resumed his dictation. Another time that he lost his temper was when he questioned me about my role in our group. "Who was the leader of this group?" he asked. I answered that no one had been appointed as leader, but that I had taken a leading part in organising our group. After growling again for a minute, he remarked with great heat: "Do you know what punishment you are going to get for all this? You will spend the best part of your life in prison." However, I think, he was rather assuaged when I convinced him that we were firmly committed to the principle of non-violence and had never even thought of indulging in any destruction of public property.

The corporal frequently made mistakes, either missing certain phrases from the long sentences which the Commandant rapidly dictated, or mis-spelling some of the big unfamiliar words, thus often annoying his boss and unwittingly drawing upon his own poor self a portion of the Commandant's wrath, which otherwise would have been directed at me.

It was usually men of the rank of corporal who acted as typists and interpreters, and being ill-educated, they proved to be not only incompetent typists but hopeless interpreters. As I learnt later from fellow prisoners, it was mainly due to interpreters that the prisoners had trouble with their interrogators. Instead of facilitating communication, the interpreter was like a thick, turbid intervening medium through which communication between the prisoner and the interrogator suffered massive distortion. The interpreter effected the first distortion when he translated the interrogator's question from Portuguese into Konkani. He effected the second distortion when he translated the prisoner's answer from Konkani into Portuguese. Finally the answer that reached the interrogator was so unexpected, or so bereft of sense that he got exasperated and began to hit the prisoner, without for a moment suspecting that the real villain was the man who was supposed to help him reach the mind of the prisoner.

It was rather smooth-sailing for me because I directly answered the Commandant's questions, and answered them promptly, without hedging, and without attempting to conceal the truth. Gradually he became more and more engrossed in the work of recording my statement in proper and impressive language, and preparing a good report of our case; and when he found that I co-operated in his work, he slowly relented towards me, and after half an hour he offered me a seat. Later on also, at police headquarters in Panjim, I came across investigating officers who being more interested in writing their reports, in good elegant language, forgot their hostility to the prisoner. From these experiences I was inclined to draw the conclusion (I do not know, how far I am justified in doing so) that for those who are sensitive to the beauties of a language, it is constitutionally impossible to be brutal.

It was a prolonged and tiring interrogation with the Commandant going into all our activities from the time I joined the freedom movement till our arrest, the previous night. And throughout the duration of the interrogation I had to remain unusually alert to answer every question to the Commandant's satisfaction. It was only after one o'clock that he completed the work and pushed the typed sheets towards me for my signature.

I returned to my prison cell thoroughly exhausted, what with the tension of the three-hour questioning, and the sleepless, anxious night before that, but feeling great relief that the first round of interrogation was over, and that I had come through it unscathed. I knew I would be questioned many times again, but that would be after the other members of our group were arrested and questioned. For the time being I could relax a bit.

I also thought of cheering up my companion Rafael in the other cell, and calling him at the door by means of the signals referred to above, I informed him that everything had gone well with me. I told him further that we might not be troubled again for some time, and that in his case they might not find it necessary to question him again. "Keep up your spirit," I called out in conclusion. He replied, to my great satisfaction, that he was feeling quite all right.

12

TWO INTERESTING PRISONERS – STUDIES IN CONTRAST

The cell I was locked in was a gloomy, dark room, a veritable "black hole" with only one small grill-opening, about a foot square, in the door. But the gloom of that dreary place was relieved by the cheerfulness of the little fellow, Atul who was always in high spirits. I do not know how unbearable I would have found those first few days of prison life, without his company, because it was the first few days of imprisonment which were really the most difficult. I derived very great encouragement from his buoyant spirit. He was either relating funny anecdotes, or with great interest questioning me about my life, or pestering me to teach him English, by orally translating simple Konkani sentences. He would go on skipping about the room while I sat on the only stone-bench in the cell and watched him or listened to him. His favourite way of relaxing was by resting his legs and hips on the stone-bench and hanging the rest of his body outside the bench, with his palms and sometimes his head touching the floor. And in that convenient position he invariably sang the same Hindi song: *Jaye to jaye kahan....* which, as far as I remember, I first heard from him. Over and over again he sang it, till it permeated our very being.

Jaye to jaye kahan?
Samjhega kaun yahan
Dard bhari dil ki juban?

(Where at all can I go? Who will here understand the painful utterance of my heart?)

Perhaps it was the only song he knew, or perhaps he had learnt it recently and could not get it out of his mind. It was a sad song – both its words and tune – and quite appropriate to our situation; but not at all in consonance with his temperament. But this sad song was the only concession that his cheerful nature allowed to the dreariness of the place. At that time I did not realise how indelibly the song was impressing itself on my mind. It was only after my release from prison, four and a half years later that I became aware of the strange power it had over me. Whenever I heard the song or its tune, I felt myself transported to that prison cell – the gloomy mood of those days once again took possession of my mind; the dark, dingy room seemed to be again enclosing me; the image of my friend, Atul seemed to rise before my eyes; and I had a vivid, a particularly vivid sensation of the smells of that prison. That song continued to affect me in that manner for many, many years; and only very slowly did the effect wear off.

On the day after our arrest, in the afternoon, my sister came to see me. I was called to the Commandant's room and was told that I could see her for just a few minutes and receive the things she brought, but could not speak to her. Then my sister was sent for. She was also informed by the Commandant that as my case was still under investigation, he could not allow anyone to speak to me, but that she could see me and go. I saw the look of great anxiety in her eyes as she glanced at me. She was worried that I might have been tortured. By a smile and a surreptitious nod I tried to convey to her that I was quite allright. The Commandant then asked to see the things she had brought for me. It was some clothes. He asked his secretary to examine them and then handed them to me; and thereupon he told my sister that it was time for her to leave. As she left, I saw that she was much consoled by this dumb visit; it really did relieve her of her anxiety.

That night they put another prisoner into our cell. It was an interesting case, not only because of the interesting story behind his arrest, but also because of the strange way in which he behaved on being locked in.

It was about eleven o'clock in the night; the whole police station was quiet by this hour and we were preparing to lie down. Suddenly we heard footsteps of three or four men coming in the corridor. They stopped in front of our cell, and then our door was thrown open. We saw that three policemen had come escorting a very decent looking gentleman, about 35 years old, strongly built and quite elegantly dressed in a safari suit and carrying a felt hat in both his hands. But what was unusual about him was that he was the very picture of misery. Even when the door was kept invitingly wide open before him, he stood like one lost, not knowing what was expected of him. The policemen seemed disinclined to be harsh with him. For some moments they stood watching him. Then a corporal among them stepped forward and stretching his hand towards the door made a slight bow to the gentleman. Finally the gentleman seemed to understand and entered the cell. But as soon as the door was closed upon him he broke down completely, and raising one hand to his face, while with the other still holding the hat, he began to sob like a child, loudly and unrestrainedly. We stood aghast. For both of us there was something unpleasant, something shocking in the sight of an adult weeping so loudly. Feeling outraged I took hold of his arm and shaking him, at first rather gently, went on questioning him: "What is wrong? Why do you weep? Tell us. Is it simply because you are arrested?" But when he neither answered nor stopped weeping, I started shaking him more roughly, and went on scolding him: "Stop it. Are you not ashamed to cry like a little child? Are we not also in prison like you?" And we both took hold of him one on each side and led him to the stone-bench and seated him thereon. He gradually calmed down, and for the first time looked at us with some surprise, and then began to speak, "I am innocent," he spluttered. "How can they think I am against them when so many of the Portuguese police officers have been my friends? Many times have I gone for hunting with them in the jungles of Sanguem."

From what the gentleman told us, it appeared that he was arrested merely on suspicion because some of his village friends were somehow involved in the freedom movement. What had hurt him most was that the police officer, who arrested him was, as he claimed, a friend with whom he had often "gone hunting in the jungles of Sanguem." When he came to this part of the story, this brave hunter gave a sob, and had to be administered a little rough jerk in the arm, in order to prevent him from breaking out into regular sobbing.

I could not be expected to feel great affinity for this gentleman with his Portuguese proclivities; but being a fellow prisoner he certainly had some claim on our sympathy. As older denizens of the cell we did everything in our power to make the gentleman feel a little comfortable in the dreary place, and to raise his low spirits. And little Atul, as an experienced prisoner gave this big, sturdy hunter encouraging tips on coping with prison life – It was indeed an ironical situation! With the intention of consoling him, I told the gentleman that as he was not involved in any nationalist activity, I was sure, he would be released soon. "But," I went on, "You need not be ashamed of being in prison. I am against Portuguese rule in Goa, and I am proud to be in prison." That quite scandalised him, and he ceased showing interest in the matter. The gentleman himself was quite narrow in his sympathies. He lamented his lot; but he did not ask either Atul or me about our lot. The next day he was separated from us. I did not see him again, nor did I hear of him. I think he was questioned and soon released – to resume his hunting with his Portuguese friends in the jungles of Sanguem.

Three days after our arrest Rafael and I were told to pack our things and get ready to move: we were to be transferred to the police headquarters at Panjim. I knew that eventually we would be taken there and further interrogated, but I had not expected it so soon. Now once again I was gripped with anxiety: what sort of investigating officers would we face? How would we be treated? In what conditions would we be kept? There was also the regret about Atul. Though I was sorry to lose his company, still I had hoped that the little fellow would be released before we were moved. I knew he had the indomitable spirit to go on bearing imprisonment, yet I felt that it was cruel to keep such a small boy in prison.

As I waited for the police guards to take us away, Atul and I had our last talk. I told him I was sure he would be released soon as he was too young to be kept in jail. "But," I continued, "Don't get involved in the freedom movement again. Finish your studies and then you can think of the movement; that is, if the Portuguese are still here." His only words of regret at parting were, "I wish they had kept you here longer."

I did not see Atul again. Even after my release from jail, four and half years later, or after liberation, a couple of years still later, I just could not trace him. Perhaps after his release his parents had taken him out of Goa to prevent him from getting into trouble again. But I always remembered this courageous boy as a fine example of the triumph of the human spirit over adversity.

13

AT POLICE HEADQUARTERS

In the Midst of Tribulations Kindness from a Stranger

For some time Rafael and I were together again, not only during the jeep journey, but also in the first cell at police headquarters where we were kept for some hours. This room was used as a transit cell, and was so small, that it was no better than a cage. Another feature that gave it the appearance of a cage was that in place of the entire front wall, there was an iron grill door, in consequence of which the inmates seated on the floor, were, like some caged wild animals, exposed to the view of all who passed in the corridor.

As a rule, the police authorities did not mix political prisoners with criminal prisoners. But sometimes the mix-up occurred, in most cases immediately after transfer of prisoners from various police stations to the headquarters. In this particular cage of a room, we were locked up with another prisoner, a truck driver, who was charged with driving rashly and knocking down and seriously injuring an old man. The driver tried to convince us that it was not his fault; but we were not convinced. The callous way in which he described the whole incident showed the man to be quite heartless. We found his company quite oppressive, and eagerly awaited our removal to some other cell. Fortunately for us in a few hours we both were taken away, each to a separate cell.

We had passed comparatively quiet days at Mapusa police station. But here at Panjim police headquarters it was a life of tribulations for prisoners. All the serious cases, both criminal and political were brought here from other police stations, so that there was a constant stream of prisoners pouring in. The interrogations went on for weeks, and in the case of political prisoners particularly, for months, with the investigating officers using all sorts of methods in dealing with the prisoners. The nature of the methods used depended not only upon the nature of the cases, but also on the nature of the investigating officers themselves, some of whom were quite vicious, the most vicious of them all being the notorious *agente* Monteiro. During the peak years of the movement, i.e. the years 1955, 1956 and even 1957, all the cells at Panjim were filled to their capacity and the total number of prisoners at police headquarters at any time during those years was not less than a hundred. A political prisoner who faced the prospect of being sent to trial, spent two to three months at police headquarters answering interrogations, and during that period he went through nerve-racking experiences – he was locked up in dark, crowded and suffocating cells; he was sometimes a victim of police brutalities; he heard prisoners being tortured, and he saw prisoners who were badly tortured; he met all sorts of prisoners, each of whom had his own tale of woe. It was only when his investigation was completed that he had a chance of being transferred to another prison – to Altinho, or to Aguada Fort, or to Reis Magos Fort, where life was easier.

I was put in a cell already containing one inmate, another non-political, a young man from Daman. The very first thing that I noticed on looking at this man was that he had a peculiar unhealthy pallor, though otherwise he did not seem to be suffering from any physical ailment. His whole appearance was rather spectral. It was as if the man had risen from the grave or had returned after spending years of his life in deep dungeons. However, he was of a friendly disposition, and talked quite freely about the trouble that had landed him into prison. It was as he called it "an accident." How long had he been in prison? "Four years," he said.

I was quite shaken by that answer. For the first time I was meeting a man who had spent long years in jail. No doubt we had come prepared to remain in jail; but so far, remaining in jail had been for me only an idea. What would be the actual experience of years of imprisonment? Here, I thought, I was seeing the image that embodied that experience. It was quite shocking to realise that a man could be reduced to the state of a spectre by long incarceration. This was what happened, I thought, to a man shut out from God's world. Cut off from the sources of vitality he lost his natural, healthy colour of life, and acquired the unnatural, morbid pallor of decay.

The young man's unhealthy appearance might not have been entirely due to his four years of imprisonment. (Though prisoners deprived of salubrious sunlight for long periods of time, as I learnt from experience, did acquire an unsightly, unhealthy pallor). But in my state of agitation, I imagined that every prisoner would necessarily be reduced to this terrible state by years of imprisonment.

Then, I was thinking, what about the inner springs of life – those springs that give rise to hope, courage, loyalty, sincerity and all the other noble impulses that make a man a worthy human being? Would those springs also be dried up in the course of long, barren years of imprisonment, so that one was left a hollow shell of a man? I vowed then that I would not let the weight of the long years of imprisonment I might have to go through, to crush out my humanity; I vowed I would not allow stone walls to imprison my spirit; I vowed that jail would really prove to be a hermitage which would educate my spirit.

My companion from Daman then went into the details of his story. Four years before he was a constable in the Portuguese police at Daman, and had already served a number of years when the "accident" occurred. Two of his fellow constables, (both young), were involved in a violent quarrel and almost came to blows. Sergio intervened and tried to separate them, when one of the antagonists who very much resented Sergio's intervention, suddenly whipped out his revolver and shot at him, but missed him. Sergio was then in self-defence compelled to use his revolver. The result was that the man was killed, and Sergio was charged with homicide. He was tried by the High Court in Goa and convicted for ten or twelve years. He had filed an appeal against the sentence before the Portuguese Supreme Court, and was awaiting its verdict.

That was Sergio's version of the "accident" that had landed him in prison. I was inclined to believe it as substantially true, for Sergio did not have anything of the murderer in him. On only one point was I disposed to doubt the truth of his narrative: that his intervention in the quarrel had been entirely disinterested. From certain details that Sergio divulged I concluded that one of the antagonists was Sergio's friend and that Sergio had intervened on his behalf. But, I was convinced that he had not intended homicide; the shot that had proved fatal had certainly been fired inadvertently.

I liked to believe that Sergio was innocent because I found him quite considerate and sympathetic, and on the whole, as I judged, a good man. Initially I had been rather prejudiced against him: the prejudice having originated in the aversion I felt for his spectral appearance, and being reinforced by his story. But the very first evening in that cell I had an experience of his kindness which compelled me to revise my opinion of the man.

I did not have any bedding with me, neither a mat nor a bedsheet, as it had not struck me to provide myself with these things at the time of our arrest. (It was only some days later that my sister came with the bedding). In Mapusa I had managed somehow to sleep on the stone-bench. But this cell was entirely bare except for Sergio's canvas cot. When it was time for us to sleep, I spread one of my spare shirts on the floor, and prepared myself to sleep on it, using the other spare clothes for a pillow. Sergio, noticing what I was doing, at once stopped me. "If you sleep like that on the cold floor, you will have a very stiff back by morning," he said. And taking from his cot a spare canvas sheet and a bedsheet he passed them to me.

I was indebted to him for other little acts of kindness, and in consequence, I overcame my initial aversion to him, and came to like him considerably. However, there was one matter on which we remained poles apart – the freedom movement. He had no sympathy for the movement, stubbornly holding the opinion that the Portuguese regime in India (Goa, Daman & Diu) would last eternally. After the first embarrassing exchange of views on the subject we avoided by a tacit understanding all reference to the freedom struggle in our talk. But I always gave him credit for being so considerate to me inspite of the division between us. Later, after our separation, when I learnt from some other prisoners that Sergio had been acquitted by the Portuguese Supreme Court and had been released, I was genuinely happy on his account, even though the thought that he had once again donned the hateful police uniform left a little unpleasantness in the mind.

Before the night passed I had quite an unnerving experience. A little after midnight our sleep was suddenly broken by a violent rattling of the cell door. When it was thrown open, two police officers accompanied by three constables entered our cell and began to search the room, unceremoniously turning over all our things. They confiscated Sergio's little pen-knife and his glass tumbler and water bottle. Then with pliers they tore out the iron nails from the walls. After they left, Sergio began to make guesses that something serious must have happened in one of the cells. He hailed the passing sentry with whom he was on friendly terms, and obtained the following report: A prisoner locked in solitary confinement in a very small room had tried to commit suicide by cutting his throat with an old shaving blade which he had obtained from a sentry, on the pretext of paring his nails. About midnight the sentry had heard groans issuing from the cell, and on looking into it had seen the prisoner lying in a pool of blood. The man had then been removed to a hospital in a serious condition. That was all the information we could get. What had prompted the man to attempt suicide? Was it because he had been tried and awarded a long sentence? Or was it because he found imprisonment wholly unbearable? Or could it be that the man was of an unsound mind? We could not get answers to these questions. Nor could we later find out whether the man survived or succumbed to the self-inflicted injury. Like some of the instances of suffering that one meets with in prison, this one also remained anonymous.

The second night also I had another frightful experience. These frightful occurrences at night affected one much more than in the daytime, specially when a prisoner was new to these experiences. Sergio and I had lain down about 10.30 p.m. and gradually drifted into sleep. Half an hour later I was jolted out of my sleep by loud screams coming from somewhere nearby. In the stillness of the night and in my sleepy state those screams sounded quite unearthly, and at first I could not make out what they meant. They ceased abruptly as I raised myself and sat listening bolt upright. Some moments later they recommenced louder then before; and then I realised that it was a prisoner being beaten in one of the rooms close by. The screams came intermittently four or five times, indicating that the prisoner was questioned and beaten. I found myself, in my great agitation, pacing up and down in the room. My movements now woke up Sergio, who also sat up and listened, though he was rather cool about the whole thing. He explained in a matter-of-fact way that in some serious and urgent cases the interrogation of prisoners commenced immediately after the arrests which were usually effected at night. Besides, he added, some investigating officers were in the habit of conducting interrogations at night.

Soon after the screams had ceased and stillness had again descended upon the whole police premises Sergio was once again fast asleep; but I could not get sleep for the rest of the night. Those screams seemed to haunt me not only that night but for many days and nights after. Later on, I heard many times again prisoners being beaten both in the daytime and at night; but it was something which always disturbed my mind, something which I could never get used to, or even regard with resignation. Every time my spirit seemed to rise in indignation at this inhuman police brutality.

The Portuguese police were undoubtedly quite brutal. But the Portuguese, as a people, being by temperament incapable of that cool and calculated cruelty which is found in some other races, the brutality of their police was of the haphazard, impulsive kind which they showed when opposed, or thwarted, or perplexed. Salazar's regime was considered as crypto-fascist, but its police never developed those refined and sophisticated methods of torture which were the speciality of the Fascist and Nazi police; nor did they use any complex instruments of torture. Their only instruments of inflicting pain were rubber truncheons and wooden batons. But that is not to suggest that the Portuguese police did not injure their prisoners when they manhandled them. During those three years of the peak of the freedom struggle, there were hundreds of prisoners who were beaten so badly that for weeks and even for months they could not move; there were scores of cases of victims who sustained serious permanent injuries and were disabled for life; and finally there were at least some cases of prisoners being beaten to death.

14

INTERROGATION RESUMED

I Meet an Unusual Police Investigator

After two days of anxious anticipation I was finally called for interrogation. A police guard came with a slip of paper to our cell and reading out my name asked me to dress up and come with him. Already a little unnerved by the unpleasant experiences of the past two days I was apprehensive about the kind of investigating officer I would meet. As I was putting on my clothes, Sergio whispered to me, "You are lucky! The officer you are going to is a good man." After being so long at police headquarters, he knew which officer was attended by which guard.

The investigating officer was busy attending to his papers as I was ushered into the room, and for a few moments I was free to observe him. He was middle-aged, rather short, but broad-shouldered and powerfully built. His face was rather enigmatic, but anyhow, I thought there was no softness in it. As he raised his head from his papers, I greeted him politely. He was on the point of answering my greeting, when instead he looked at me rather severely and then frowned, and finally raising his hand towards me and turning his head towards the guard, said, "How is that you bring him here in that state?" It took me some time to understand what it was in my state that had annoyed him. There was a week's growth of hair on my face which must have given me a sickly appearance. "Take him to the barber," he ordered.

I was hastily taken to the police barber and shaved, and then brought back. The officer passed a surveying glance over me, and now finding me in a presentable state, he deigned to speak to me. He asked me to sit, and then extending an open cigarette case towards me, he said, "Do you smoke?" I was astonished. I had never expected such a friendly gesture from an investigating officer towards a political prisoner. Only after I thanked him and said I didn't smoke, did he himself light a cigarette and set to work in a business like manner. But before proceeding with the interrogation proper, he said that he would like to make one thing clear to me; that he wanted nothing but the truth from me. Of course, I had nothing to hide, and so I got on very well with him.

From the papers that he referred to while questioning me, I could make out that some members of our group were already arrested and questioned. When he found that all my answers tallied with and confirmed what my associates had given in their statements, and what I myself had given in my statement at Mapusa, he developed great confidence in me, and readily accepted whatever I stated. I came away from the interrogation quite elated. It was our good fortune that our case was being dealt with by a police officer who was incapable of being brutal towards prisoners. He was benign beyond all expectations that one could have of a police officer. He was indeed a gentleman.

15

A THREE MONTH ORDEAL

An Account of Life in Panjim Police Prison

That evening of the fourth day I was taken to another cell and I parted from Sergio, never to see him again. This cell was quite big, but was overcrowded, dingy and dirty. There were about twenty-five prisoners in it with hardly enough space for all to lie down at night. The prisoners spent their waking hours sitting on mats spread on the floor, their backs leaning against the wall, chatting, disputing, playing improvised cards and draughts. The room had only two small windows: one a grill opening in the front door and another small window in the back wall, and it was dark and stuffy inside – so stuffy that prisoners without any exertion sweated most of the time. For anyone coming fresh into the cell the odour of sweat and of stale air was quite nauseating; but so surprising are the powers of human adaptation that prisoners soon learnt to tolerate and to live in those almost unbearable conditions.

I lived in that cell for about three months; that is for almost the total period that I was kept at police headquarters; and I found that period of my imprisonment the most painful. So I feel the conditions in that cell merit a little more detailed description. The interior surfaces of the cell walls were coated with some substance like tar; and constant and prolonged contact with that coating on the walls produced on our backs a skin ailment – some eruption all over the back, which the indifferent medical treatment provided by the jail doctor could not cure. For months, prisoners suffered greatly from this eruption; we could not lie on our backs, nor could we lean against the wall while sitting. It was only after we were transferred to Altinho Prison that the eruption gradually subsided.

Sometimes, an inmate of our cell would be taken for questioning and would be brought in badly beaten. There were two or three investigating officers who were well known for the pleasure they took in beating prisoners, the most sadistic of them being, of course, Monteiro. And to which interrogator a prisoner was being taken, would be known by the identity of the guard who came for the prisoner. When a prisoner was being taken to some cruel interrogator, the other prisoners would, with concern on their faces, surround him as he dressed up, and would whisper words of encouragement as he left the cell. They would then take turns watching at the grill-window awaiting the return of the prisoner. When he appeared they would gauge the state of his agony from his face. A badly-beaten prisoner came with a look of extreme exhaustion on his face; or sometimes in the case of severe injuries, the face would be distorted with the pain which the prisoner was trying to bear. When the door was opened the prisoner would take a few unsteady steps inside the cell and would then collapse, the other prisoners trying to catch him before he fell to the floor. Sometimes a prisoner would faint as soon as he reached the cell and we had to use all the therapeutic arts at our disposal to revive him.

Once a badly beaten prisoner fainted and tumbled down in a heap in the corridor near the door, as it was being opened by the guard. The sight of the fallen, unconscious prisoner lying in the corridor infuriated the police sergeant who was on duty and who happened to be near-by. What followed was a kind of surrealistic scene of cruelty. The sergeant rushed at the fallen man shouting to the guard to throw him inside the cell, and then with great frenzy he went on kicking the prostrate figure, kicked and shoved him into the cell, while some of the prisoners near the door stretched their hands and tried to grab the unconscious man and pull him inside the cell. I shall never forget that incident. The scene is etched on my memory. It was a kind of a cruel revelation to my young mind about a particular human perversity – the arousal of sadistic impulses in certain persons on seeing their opponent fallen and helpless.

At times we had two or three such badly beaten prisoners in our cell. It was most depressing to see those men lie helplessly on the floor for weeks together. Their sufferings were really unbearable. The least movement was a torture to them. Sometimes they could not move their hands to eat and so we had to feed them. We also had great difficulty making them get up in the morning which they did unwillingly and with a lot of groaning. There would be black and blue spots of congealed blood all over their bodies; we had to go on massaging them with oil for many weeks to restore proper circulation of blood. In certain cases, even when the external injuries healed, some internal effects of injuries remained which troubled them all their life.

It took a prisoner some time to adapt himself to the harsh conditions in prison, particularly the harsh conditions that prevailed at police headquarters. It was not merely a question of getting used to the great discomforts of jail life; that was not so difficult. But the brutalities and sufferings that one saw around had a tremendous demoralising impact on one's mind, an impact that shook a person to the core of his being. Undoubtedly this impact was greater on young and sensitive minds. Finally the result of this impact manifested itself in one's health.

From the time of my arrest I had very little appetite for food. I could not eat even one-third of the food given to each prisoner. In the beginning I thought it was because prison food was bad. Soon after being brought to Panjim I noticed that I was losing weight. And I went on losing weight for about a month, till finally, as I noted with concern, I was considerably emaciated. But gradually things changed. I learnt to face every tribulation of prison life with a certain degree of equanimity; by and by I developed a kind of stoic fortitude to the harsh reality of prison life. And slowly I recovered my appetite. It had not been the fault of prison food; it was tolerably good. At least it was allright for me, as I had been brought up the hard way and had never been finicky about food. And then slowly I began to increase weight, till within a couple of months I was almost my former self. Some other prisoners told me of having gone through the same process of losing weight in the beginning and then slowly regaining it.

But naturally one could not adapt oneself to prison life to the extent of feeling comfortable in jail. Imprisonment is an unnatural state, as unnatural as that of a bird destined for the freedom of the air being put in a cage. It is the loss of the most basic freedom, the creature-freedom of physical movement on God's earth. In this respect a man imprisoned is reduced to a state worse than that of animals. However well-fed a prisoner may be, however well-protected from heat and cold, he feels even in his sleep a certain constraint, a certain distress deep down within him, in the very marrow of his bones. Imprisonment with its loss of that basic freedom can hurt and degrade man at a deep level. It is only his moral and spiritual efforts that can help him to triumph over that damage and degradation.

16

SOME LIGHT INTERLUDES

The jail doctor came to see us once a week. He was from Daman and spoke Konkani with a funny pronunciation and intonation. He was impressive-looking with a well-groomed goatee-beard, and always elegantly dressed, usually in a cream coloured sharkskin suit. But his elegance ended with his outward look and his clothes – for he was quite vulgar by nature. What struck a prisoner most about this worthy disciple of Hippocrates was the surprising contrast between his impressive look and the unpalatable language that flowed from his mouth. He was the most foul-mouthed doctor that I ever saw. When speaking to prisoners, he would seize every opportunity of larding his ordinary speech with coarse expressions and obscene innuendos. The only redeeming feature about his vulgarity was that his coarse language was not prompted by anger or ill-will towards the prisoners. It was just a part of his nature, presumably.

How competent this doctor was as a physician we had no means of knowing because he treated none of the prisoners' ailments other than the injuries inflicted by police investigators, and for these he prescribed no other treatment than the application of iodine tincture. He was never seen using the stethoscope on any prisoner, or touching any prisoner with his hands. He would only take an indifferent look at the injury of the prisoner and then call out to his compounder, "Joaquim, apply the tincture on him," and then strut off to the next prison cell. Joaquim, a young fellow would then amuse himself with his make-shift cotton brush drawing geometrical designs with the tincture on the bodies of prisoners. Perhaps, the doctor could not be much blamed for not providing better medical care to prisoners; for certainly the police authorities would not have looked with favour on their doctor taking much interest in the health and well being of political prisoners.

One matter of satisfaction for me about this cell was that almost all the inmates here were political prisoners with whom I felt great ideological and emotional affinity. For the first time I was in a cell where I met so many patriots. A few of them were known to me having met me outside while working for the movement. Among these was Kantak, the Lyceum student with whom I had climbed the wild Ghats to attend the meeting at Kundal. It was a real consolation to meet in jail those patriots known to me. There was a notable sense of solidarity among all these prisoners. This solidarity expressed itself in the way prisoners showed their concern when a badly beaten prisoner was brought in: laughter and fun would be suppressed and talk would be subdued. Perhaps it will be difficult for people who have not been in similar circumstances to understand what great moral support a prisoner in his sufferings derived from the close presence of fellow prisoners who were devoted to the same cause and who suffered for the same cause. Besides, there were other tangible consolations that prisoners derived from one another. I always found that political prisoners sympathised with one another, shared their things with one another and helped one another in whatever way they could. I can imagine how unbearable life would be to a political prisoner, were he to be kept all the time in solitary confinement or to be put in the company of criminals.

How did the prisoners spend their time? They talked to one another, they exchanged information about the political situation in various parts in Goa, they discussed the prospects of the freedom movement, they shared with one another their dream of an early freedom to Goa. And many of them went on playing improvised games.

Only one prisoner had a book – some book by the philosopher Leibnitz, I forget its title. It was the only book in the cell. I suppose it was duly censored and brought in. Its owner was a young fellow who was interested not in reading but in playing draughts. And no one else showed the least interest in the book. I think the person who sent this book by Leibnitz, of all the books in the world, must have intended to inflict some punishment on the young fellow; for Leibnitz, I suppose, is not an interesting philosopher even to those who are fond of reading. Not having anything else to read, I started to read the book, and doggedly went on reading page after page. I cannot pretend that at that young age I understood all Leibnitz's philosophy, but his account of "windowless monads" made me feel gloomy. We were already shut up in a dreary place which might be aptly described as a "windowless monad", and then over and above that to think that the whole Universe might be composed of small closed-in entities called "windowless monads", that each one of us might be a "windowless monad" hopelessly shut within oneself, was quite depressing indeed. I wanted to put away the book, but new ideas had always fascinated me, specially far-fetched ideas, even though they might be pessimistic. So I read the book from cover to cover and then again read parts of it, with the result that for months I was haunted by the depressing idea of the "windowless monad."

One of the young prisoners who had interrupted his studies to join the freedom movement, but who was still eager for intellectual self-improvement, wished me to teach him a little more of English. How to teach English without any text-book, without pen and paper? We made a beginning with the oral method, but could not make much headway. But the young fellow was quite resourceful. Prisoners sometimes used to receive from their families things packed in cardboard boxes. Some of these discarded boxes were lying about in the cell. The young fellow got from each side of the box two or three sheets by separating the different layers. These sheets we called our 'papyrus'. Then he procured from some prisoner a stub of a pencil. And to my great delight, with these simple aids he improved in English considerably during the three months we were together in that cell. His example was an inspiration to me. I also decided that I would make good use of the years I might spend in jail.

There were certain episodes that in the midst of our dreary prison life came like comic interludes, or rather like tragi-comic interludes. In our cell there was a prisoner who was stark mad. He did not talk to anyone or take the least notice of anyone. Clad in dirty rags, he lay listlessly the whole day on the bare floor. Obviously he had lost interest in everything except food which he ate when placed before him. When we were taken out in the morning we had to drag him out physically, for a bath or a wash. The man was so withdrawn into himself, so oblivious of the world around him that he might be considered a veritable Leibnitz's "windowless monad." But the interesting thing about this prisoner was that he had been arrested as a political offender. I had read of political opponents in totalitarian regimes being dubbed as madmen, and persecuted by being shut up in lunatic asylums. But this prisoner had the dubious distinction of being perhaps the only madman in the world who had been branded as a political offender and harassed by being jailed. And the Portuguese police in Goa deserved the dubious credit of executing this unique gaffe.

And the story behind his arrest was interesting too. Some of the prisoners in our cell had known the man slightly outside – had seen him going about in the streets of Panjim. They said that he had not always been so dumb as he was now. While going about he used to stop occasionally, and, looking upwards, he used to gesticulate violently and speak vehemently. I am inclined to believe that his behaviour was reasonable that there was some method in his madness. He must have found that Fate had been unjust to him, and by his angry gestures and speech, he must have been directing his protests and complaints towards Heaven.

But one day, as some of our fellow prisoners related, it so happened that the man came in front of some government building over which the Portuguese flag was flying, and standing right under the flag, he raised both his voice and his hands and made his usual protest against Heaven. An over-scrupulous police officer, fresh from Portugal, watched his actions and concluded that the man was abusing the Portuguese flag and that, hence, he must be an Indian nationalist, an enemy of Portugal, and so forth. Thereupon he arrested him and brought him to police headquarters.

The investigating officer who dealt with his case tried to question him, but the man, upon his arrest, had closed himself like a clam. By then he must have realised the futility of all speech, and he scorned to demand justice from men when Heaven itself had been deaf to his protests. For a long time the investigating officer tried to puzzle out what the man was. Finally, after two months, it dawned upon the perceptive officer that the man's mind was preoccupied with matters quite other than conspiracies against Portuguese rule. And he ordered the man's release.

When a guard came with the release order and called out his name, the man did not respond at all. When we told him he was being released, and tried to raise him on his legs, he resisted with all his might. Finally some of us caught hold of him, carried him out of the cell and placed him in the corridor. From there he started walking mechanically towards the main gate.

17

TRIBUTE TO AN ENIGMATIC ENEMY

My interrogation seemed to drag on interminably. Most of the members of our group were now in police custody and they were being questioned one after the other by the same investigating officer. And after each one was questioned, I was called, and my statement confirming what they had stated was recorded. That was how my interrogation went on and on till the whole case of our group was completed, which took over two months. But in all that period, none of our group was ill-treated by our investigating officer. Nor did I hear of any other prisoner being ill-treated by him. In fact, the man, on account of his decency, had become something of an enigma to the prisoners who were interrogated by him. Some of them tried to explain his behaviour by the hypothesis that his sympathies were not with Salazar's regime, and that he belonged to the secret opposition in Portugal. But there could be a simpler explanation: That he was inherently a decent man, a good man who by mistake had landed into the police department.

As for myself, each time I met him, I had a better opinion of him. One quality in him, which in particular I liked was his love for the beauty of language. As the file of our case accumulated into over a hundred typed foolscap pages, I had the feeling that the only interest which kept alive his enthusiasm for dictating those hundred pages was that his work afforded him the opportunity of fine self-expression; he seemed to take our whole case like a grand exercise in composition. Before dictating a sentence, he would carefully compose it and then say it aloud to see how it sounded; sometimes he would halt and search for an appropriate expression, sometimes he would correct himself. There was perfect understanding between him and his secretary who used to begin typing a sentence only when it was dictated with a tone of finality. Many times when he hit upon a particularly striking phrase or composed a particularly impressive sentence, he would look up at me questioningly. At such times I was very much tempted to nod my approval; but then, I thought, for a prisoner, that would be taking undue liberty with his investigating officer. But by a certain look, I tried to convey to him that I admired his felicity of expression.

But the finest memory that I cherish of this good man is of those few moments when he seemed to form a good opinion of me, his 'enemy.' It came about in this way: One of the members of our group was the son of a man who held an important position in the Portuguese establishment. As such, he was not arrested but only summoned for questioning. Of course, if he had admitted that he had in any way participated in the freedom movement, or even that he desired the freedom of Goa, he would have been detained and brought to trial. But the young man now realising that the prospect he faced was imprisonment, repented having worked for the movement, and denied all association with us. Hence I was brought and made to confront him. This was the only time when I was brought to confront a member of our group, because, in this case only our respective statements entirely contradicted each other's. The investigating officer selected a relevant statement of mine, given much earlier, one which related to the young man, and having read it aloud, he turned to me and said, "Do you still maintain what you have stated here?" "Yes," I said. Then the officer turned to the young man and asked? "Is all that he says here true?" "It is all false," the young man said, "He lies."

The officer once again turned to me and said, "What have you to say to that?"

I was expecting that in this case, naturally, the officer's sympathy would be with the young man who was not going against Portuguese sovereignty. At the risk of arousing his anger, I said, with considerable warmth. "On this point, whatever I had to say, I have already given in this statement here. I am sorry, Sir, I have nothing more to add to that."

"But he says you lie!"

"I have nothing to say to that either" I said, now fully expecting him to explode at me. But instead, the officer stared at me for about ten seconds, as if he were seeing me in a new light. A faint, confidential sort of smile spread over his face. Then finally pointing to the young man and grinning broadly he said to me, "You wanted to bring about a revolution with such men?" I took it as a great compliment from a worthy 'enemy.'

Then, in a neutral sort of voice, the officer went on questioning the young man and recording his statement just as he gave it. He left me sitting there and completely ignored me throughout the questioning. I did not understand why he did not send me to my cell. I had a feeling that he wanted me to see that the recording of that statement was a mere matter-of-form to him, that he was concerned neither with its truth nor its falsehood. On completing his statement, he said to the young man curtly, "You can go now." After that his mood seemed to change. He became serious, almost sad. A minute later he lifted his head and called to the guard to take me to my cell.

18

I AM QUESTIONED BY THE DREADED AGENTE MONTEIRO

During those three months I was at police headquarters, I was also called for questioning four or five times, by other investigating officers. When you were called by a different interrogator, you went with trepidation in your heart, because you did not know what the officer wanted from you and how he would treat you. But it turned out, in most of the cases, I was wanted by other interrogators only because my statement was needed to fill certain lacunae in the case-reports of certain prisoners not belonging to our group. The activities of these freedom fighters had been somehow connected with our activities, and in their statement they had made certain references to me or to our group. The interrogators now checked and confirmed those references by recording my statement in that regard. These were generally matters of detail to which the interrogators did not attach much importance; and that is why I had no trouble even from some of the brutal interrogators. They questioned me for about fifteen minutes in an off-hand manner and then dismissed me.

But the worst interrogator I faced was the notorious monster, Monteiro. He was dreaded by every prisoner, because by this time his reputation as a cruel brute was well established. With his brutal beatings he had maimed scores of prisoners and he had beaten to death at least four or five prisoners, among them a man from my village, Assonora.[1]

1. [Bala Mapari of Assonora was arrested in connection with the assault on Assonora police post, early in 1955, and was tortured to death by *Agente* Monteiro.]

Monteiro was a *mestizo* (mixed breed), fair, rather tall, and powerfully built, quite handsome-looking, but with a cold, cruel glint in his eyes. We used to see him often walk past our cell with a swaggering stride, followed by his six to eight assistants all young mestizo ruffians, whom we used to call his "hounds". They reminded one of a pack of hounds, because beside their chief they appeared quite small, and like dogs they followed closely at his heels. They always accompanied him when he went by jeep on his rounds all over Goa, arresting people. And when he interrogated prisoners, it was these "hounds" who took hold of the prisoner and threw him on a stone bench and pinned him there, while Monteiro went on beating him with a rubber truncheon or a wooden baton.

What impelled Monteiro to do all this horrible work so diligently? It was not so much loyalty to his Portuguese masters. He was an adventurer in the worst sense of the word – an adventurer with the instincts of a gangster. And like every man of that type he wished to make an easy and a fast buck. There were reports circulating all over Goa that he used to arrest innocent young men of well-to-do families and then demand large sums of money from their parents for their release. And the others, from whose relatives he could not expect money, he beat up mercilessly thereby pleasing his bosses in the police department and gaining the reputation of a 'hero' in the Portuguese establishment.

One day, after I had spent about two months at Panjim, one of Monteiro's 'hounds' came to our cell and called out my name. I was surprised because Monteiro had never been concerned with our case; he used to deal mostly with the cases of prisoners who were in the armed movement; and secondly, I knew that our case-report was on the point of being completed and sent up to the Military Tribunal. But whatever the reason for my being wanted, I knew what to expect, and I braced myself for the ordeal.

As I began to dress up many of the prisoners came around, someone handing me my shirt, another my trousers, still another a comb, some of them murmuring, "Don't lose courage." In two minutes I was ready and left the cell.

Fear had gripped my mind as soon as my name was called out. However, strangely enough as I entered Monteiro's room and went and stood before his table, I felt myself unexpectedly calm and composed. I noticed that his other "hounds" were not in the room, and, the one who escorted me also left the room at once. But perhaps they could be called at a moment's signal. As Monteiro began to speak I saw that he was quite drunk, and that he appeared rather exhausted, though mentally he was quite alert. It was already afternoon, and may be, I was the last piece of business he was attending to before going away for lunch.

He began by asking me whether I had worked for the movement in Aldona and the surrounding places. I admitted that. Then abruptly he demanded, "Now tell me who are the people in the violent movement in that area." I replied that being in the non-violent movement, I had no contact whatsoever with those in the armed movement, and hence I did not know if there were any such people in that area.

"No," he said, "While going about your work you must have met people who are in that movement, and I want their names."

I repeated that we in the non-violent movement had no reason to meet those belonging to the other movement, and so I was not aware of any such people in the area.

"No, I do not accept that answer," he said with rising temper. "I tell you I want those names."

When I remained silent for some time, he barked threateningly, "Do you hear?"

I could only say, "I am sorry, I do not know of any such people."

At this he suddenly got up flourishing a wooden rib which had lain concealed by his side behind the table, and with that he went on hitting me. While leaving the cell I had resolved not to cry out in pain however much he beat me, not being sure, of course, how far I would be able to stick to that resolution. Now, to my surprise, I found that I could bear the pain of the blows without even much flinching. Fear seems to play a strange trick on a person; it disables one in certain ways no doubt, but it also dulls one's sensation of pain. I received some of the blows on my hands, the rest landed on my sides. But Monteiro was really tired and hungry. Soon he was panting, and then he stopped.

"I'm letting you off now, as I have to go for lunch," he said. "I give you one day. Tomorrow I'll call you, and I'll not treat you so softly, unless I have the names at once."

My cell mates were glad that my injuries were light; all the same, with great solicitude some of them massaged the bruised spots with oil. When I told them what Monteiro wanted from me, they began to surmise that some nationalist activity must have taken place in Aldona or nearby. And in fact, after a week or so, we learnt from new prisoners that the police outpost at Aldona had been attacked by armed nationalist and all arms taken away.

The next day, with considerable fear I awaited Monteiro's call. It did not come. Still for another two or three days I expected it. But it never came. As for my injuries, they healed completely in about a fortnight.

This Monteiro who could strike terror in the hearts of people soon had his downfall, and even before Portuguese rule in Goa ended, men, whom he had injured and maimed, had the satisfaction of knowing that this great bully was brought low and made to bite the dust. For a time he had been able to pose as a staunch and loyal subject of Salazar while amassing a fortune by blackmailing people and extorting money from them, and at the same time indulging his sadistic impulses. But it was the investigating officers who had come from Portugal after the freedom movement reached its peak who saw through his game and unmasked him. It was also reported that the good officer who dealt with our case, played an important role in this work. Monteiro was put under arrest and taken to Portugal. And it was rumoured that the police there gave him a dose of the same medicine that he used to administer to Goan prisoners. He would not easily reveal where he had concealed or invested his ill-gotten wealth, and so the interrogators there beat him to make him confess – beat him so much, it was rumoured, that they left him with a permanent limp.

19

TRANSFER TO ALTINHO PRISON

When the cells at police headquarters used to get crowded as a result of continued arrests, the authorities used to transfer those prisoners whose case-reports were completed, or were about to be completed. to other prisons, particularly to Altinho prison, which was quite near to police headquarters. It was only at a later stage – that is usually after prisoners were tried, or at least their police reports already sent to the Military Tribunal – that they were removed to the more permanent prisons of Aguada Fort, or Reis Magos Fort. About two and a half months after our arrest, I understood that our interrogation was over (as, for quite some time we were not taken for questioning), and I began to look forward to be transferred to Altinho along with the other prisoners whose interrogations were over. It was only after I had spent three months at Panjim, that finally a large number of us were transported by closed Black Maria to Altinho.

This Altinho prison was formerly a government mental hospital, which the exigencies of those times had compelled the Portuguese government to convert into a prison.[1] It comprised two separate buildings surrounded by a very high wall, insurmountable not only for mental patients, but also for political prisoners. Each building consisted of about thirty small rooms, each room being originally intended for one mental patient, but now containing five, or six or even more prisoners. So that there were more than a hundred and fifty prisoners in each building, i.e. more than three hundred prisoners in the whole of Altinho Prison.[2]

---

1. [The place is once again a mental hospital].

2. [The total number of political prisoners in Goa at this time, incarcerated in Aguada Fort. Reis Magos Fort. Altinho prison and at police headquarters might have been between eight hundred to one thousand.]

Though these rooms were too small even for five prisoners (each room was about 10 x 10 feet), they were rather well lit and well ventilated, each room having a large window opposite the door; and hence they were incomparably more comfortable than the dingy, suffocating cells at police headquarters. Our window gave a view of part of the barren compound, part of the surrounding wall, and a little part of the sky, so that we spent all the seven or eight months we were kept there without a glimpse of a tree or a plant, or even a bird, except an occasional dismal crow that happened to fly in that part of the sky.

20

WHITE AND NEGRO SENTINELS

We were still in the custody of the police because the police department was in charge of this prison; but the guarding of the prison was done by the army. There was a military garrison stationed on the premises and its soldiers used to stand sentinel at various points all around the prison. There used to be two sentries on our side of the building, and they used to walk up and down often passing by our window. Most of the soldiers of this garrison were very young conscripts, some less than twenty, some in their early twenties – all pink, chubby and childish looking. Some were quite fresh from Portugal, and these would come and stare at us with wonder in their eyes. Sometimes they would exchange impressions about us, their remarks such as *tem caras simpaticas* (= they have pleasant faces) showing that they had expected to find the "enemies of Portugal" quite savage-looking. They were still more surprised when they found that some of us could speak Portuguese, and that we were better informed about the world than themselves.

But there were some who could not, even after seeing us, believe that we might be civilised. Among these was a group of three young conscripts who came together to our window and tried to amuse themselves at our cost. Perhaps they thought that we could not converse in any civilised tongue. For two days they came and stood at the window and with funny sounds and gestures they tried to tease us like naughty boys teasing some caged animals. And both the days we watched them rather sulkily. But after that we thought of a better way of dealing with them. On the third day when they came and were about to begin their tomfoolery, all five of us greeted them cheerfully, *bom dia*! (= Good morning). They were rather taken aback. And when we tried to start a polite conversation with them in Portuguese they beat a hasty retreat in confusion and embarrassment. They did not come again to tease us. And when any one of them happened to be on sentry duty near our cell, he would walk far from our window and smile shyly at us.

Most of these soldiers were simple fellows with very little education, and very little knowledge of the world, which was surprising considering that they came from the big cities of Portugal, mainly from Lisbon and Oporto. We wondered, if Portuguese urban youth were such, what the rural fellows would be like. But though we were eager to meet them, we did not find any country youngsters among them.

However, we found most of the military fellows possessed of a friendly disposition, and without ill-will towards us. Very often we used to request the sentries to bring us books from the other cells, particularly from the cells occupied by non-Goan Indian prisoners[1] who used to receive regular supplies of books and magazines through the Egyptian Consulate at Bombay[2] Of course passing of books and other things from one cell to another, except through the official channel was against prison regulations, and the police authorities would not allow any contact between Goan and non-Goan Indian prisoners. So the sentries who tried to bring us books from the other cells ran the risk of being punished in accordance with military discipline. Even then many of them were good enough to oblige us, though some refused. The first time that we sent a sentry to the cell of Mr. N.G. Goray, he came back and said, "That fellow doesn't understand anything." Of course we had foreseen the difficulty of communication between two persons not knowing each

---

1. [Some of the prominent non-Goan Indians who had led batches of *satyagrahis* in 1955 were detained while the rest were soon deported across the border. Among those detained and now incarcerated in Altinho jail were prominent political leaders like N.G. Goray, of the erstwhile Praja Socialist Party, Madhu Limaye of the Socialist Party, and Tridib Kumar Choudhary of the Revolutionary Socialist Party. Later on, along with the Goan prisoners they were moved to Aguada Fort Prison.]

2. [Once the freedom movement had begun, India had cut off diplomatic relations with Portugal. The Egyptian government was then looking after Indian interests in Portuguese territories. The Egyptian Consul at Bombay used to make occasional trips to Goa to see the Indian prisoners, each time bringing them books and other things].

other's language; but we had been unwilling that the sentry should carry an elaborately written message, because that would make his offence still more serious. Now we took a bit of paper and wrote thereon "books" and sent the sentry again. After some time he returned with two books. With the help of that word and with his signs and gestures he had made it clear to Mr. Goray that prisoners in another cell wished to borrow books from him. Thus, thanks to the kindness of those young soldiers we borrowed many books from non-Goan prisoners, and experienced, for the first time in jail, the great pleasure of reading.

It is difficult to exaggerate the consolation that those in prison can derive from reading, particularly from great literature which has the magic power of transporting you to another world. Most of the books that we got from the non-Goan prisoners were not literature, but books on history and politics and a few on philosophy. Even then, in the absence of other books, they were not only enlightening but consoling too. And we remember with gratitude those young soldiers who were the means of providing us with that consolation in Altinho prison. It was difficult for us to get our own books in prison so long as we were in the custody of the police, because the books had to be first submitted to the police authorities for censorship, and then they would take months to reach the prisoners, if at all they reached them; for often inspite of repeated inquiries books would be irretrievably lost. It was only when we were taken to Aguada Fort and put under the care of the military, that it became easier to get our own books.

I remember two of those young soldiers specially for another act of kindness. These two were very genial fellows with frank, honest faces. They had obliged us many times by bringing us books from other cells. One evening, after dark, they both came to our window and called us rather excitedly. One of them remained in the dark by the side of the window, and seemed to be hiding something. "Have some coffee, we brought you some coffee" they said. We had some small steel tumblers which we passed through the window bars, and they filled them with coffee from some aluminium vessel. Obviously, they had stolen the coffee from the mess kitchen, and had thought of sharing it with us. When they left we began to sip the coffee – it was cold, watery and tasteless. Nevertheless, we drank it out of appreciation of their kindness to us. The poor quality of their coffee roused our curiosity about the quality of their food in general. And in course of casual conversations about their barrack life, we learnt that the Portuguese common soldiers ate food which was quite poor in quality.

A few negroes formed a part of this garrison, and some of them also used to be posted as sentries on our side of the prison. These were the last negro soldiers we saw in Goa. In fact, since the beginning of the freedom movement not many negro soldiers were brought to Goa. The reason might be that with the rise of freedom movements, first in Angola and then in Mozambique, the Portuguese authorities were not sure of the loyalties of their African troops. But in my childhood days we used to see many of them all over Goa. To us children then, they were like beings from another planet. I remember particularly the negro military teams that used to come to play football on our village grounds, fascinating us children, not only with their skill as football players, but also with their loud, childish laughter, and their lusty singing. Now as a prisoner, I was eager to know the feelings of these negroes as members of a subject race.

There were two young negroes who, when on duty often used to pass by our window. One of them was a very taciturn fellow who would not speak even when spoken to. I think it was because he was afraid of getting into trouble by speaking to us; for sentries were, in fact, forbidden to speak to prisoners. We gave him up as a hopeless case. The other fellow was a more interesting specimen. Sometimes, for the whole duration of his two-hour sentry duty he used to walk up and down and go on singing some native African song while playing on a one-stringed instrument. It was a strange, rather monotonous kind of song, with more of rhythm than melody to it, a song redolent of life in the African bush. It consisted mainly of an endlessly repeated refrain. While singing it, the man would have a faraway look in his eyes which suggested that he felt himself transported to his native land, and perhaps felt himself communing with the spirits of the African forests.

This negro was quite friendly, and when not occupied with his music, would talk to us about himself. It was he who told us that all the negroes in that garrison including himself came from Mozambique. He was not aware of any Angolan Negro being in Goa at that time. We tried to find out discreetly what he felt about Portuguese rule in Mozambique. But the man was so simple-minded that he had no political consciousness whatsoever, and his thoughts did not go beyond his basic needs. This was brought home to us when we led him to talk about South Africa, about which, we thought, every negro would feel strongly. We had expected him to condemn with great indignation the oppression of his fellow negroes in that country, but to our great surprise he said, "It is very fine in South Africa; you get flour, you get potatoes, you get everything." Many of the negroes of Mozambique lived in such primitive conditions, that their sole concern seemed to be the acquisition of the primary necessities of life. And many of them used to go as contract labour to South Africa where the economic conditions of negroes were better than in Mozambique.

But there was one negro who seemed to us truly to embody the spirit of Africa. He was a hewer of wood; and he came almost everyday near our window with a heavy axe to split logs of wood which were brought there by lorry. I think he did only the menial work of the garrison, for we never saw him doing sentry duty. He was a man of herculean strength, and he wielded the axe powerfully, splitting a thick log with one stroke, sending big splinters of wood flying all over, and setting the whole prison building resounding with the strokes of his axe. We all watched him with fascination as he came to work clad only in shorts, his countenance rather sad, his eyes always downcast. He was aware that we were watching him, but he never raised his eyes to glance at us, seeming to be indifferent to everything around except his work. He was truly an enigma to us. He appeared to be a picture of patience and forbearance. But who could say whether he was content with his lot as a hewer of wood in an alien land? Who could guess what silent stirrings moved his heart? Who could fathom the soul of this dark Hercules? I was seized with a strange notion that if I could look into his eyes, I would get a glimpse into his soul and wrest his secret; and day by day I stood at the window watching him at his work, hoping to catch his eyes. But the man, as if reluctant to reveal the secret of his soul, kept his eyes always downcast and intent on his work.

21

AFFLICTIONS AT ALTINHO

One source of distress for us here at Altinho was the insufficiency of toilets and bathrooms. There were only two toilets and two bathrooms in our building, for more than a hundred and fifty prisoners. And the police guards wanted us to rush through our morning business, because at eight o'clock in the morning there used to be a change of guard, and before that, those guards who were on duty for the night wanted to put the prisoners back in the cells, to give them tea, and finally to count them and hand over the charge to their successors. To make us hurry through the morning business the guards put every kind of pressure on us – they kept open the doors of bathrooms and toilets, they yelled at us, they abused us and cursed us, they assumed threating postures before us, they even pushed us roughly. And all this told considerably on the nerves of prisoners, specially in the beginning, when this situation was entirely new to us.

But some guards were more humane; they got up earlier and let us out earlier so that we had sufficient time. There was one Goan guard, I remember, who shouted and raged at us when his superior, a white corporal was within hearing range. It did not take us long to understand that his raging was mere "sound and fury signifying nothing" and that though apparently directed at us, it was intended for the ears of the European corporal. When the corporal was not around, he sat quietly talking to us, and he let us have our own time. It was quite amusing to see the good fellow at one monent, when the corporal was not near, talking kindly to a group of prisoners, and at the very next moment, at the approach of the corporal, springing up and shouting furiously at the same group of prisoners. Our hearts went out to this kindly dissembler.

Another trouble at Altinho was that in the summer months there was scarcity of water. During the rest of the year we used to get tap water, but in the summer months the taps ran dry and water was brought by motor tankers. Then there would not be sufficient water even for our morning needs. As for bath, it became a luxury to be enjoyed once in a few days. I remember, at one time we had to remain without bath for six days, and in consequence, it being the hot season, we felt quite sick. At such times one had almost a delirious longing to dip oneself in water, and one began daydreaming of all the cool streams and pools one had known outside. The only comfort in this situation was that our cells were rather airy, and Altinho being at a high altitude, there used to be sufficient breeze, specially in the afternoons. If these cells had been like those at police headquarters, we could imagine what torture it would be to remain without bath for days together.

22

VISITS BY THE PORTUGUESE RED CROSS AND AN ITALIAN JOURNALIST

Apart from the usual visits from close relatives allowed by the authorities once a week, we had two other unexpected visits in the course of those seven months we spent at Altinho. One was from the Portuguese branch of the Red Cross. We were astonished one afternoon to hear female voices chirping in the corridor. When our doors were opened we saw a small group of ladies, members of the Red Cross, going to each cell bearing tins of milk powder. They presented each prisoner with a half kilo tin. It was a welcome diversion; both the sudden appearance of the ladies in the prison building, and the gift of the milk powder. The milk was not only a supplement to our prison food, but its preparation provided some real diversion in the dull routine of prison life. At first we tried to drink it by just mixing it in cold water; it did not taste so good unboiled. But how to boil it? Some of our cell mates rose to the occasion and provided a solution. From the number of things that we improvised in prison, it was quite a relevation to me, inspite of my familiarity with the relevant proverb, how inventive ordinary people can be in situations of necessity. Though we were not allowed to get into prison any stove or any fuel, we were permitted the use of candles when electricity failed. Now some of our fellows prepared a fine little stove out of a tin can by cutting an appropriate hole in it with a pen knife. For fuel we used candles. This stove was so efficient that no heat from the candle was wasted. With one small candle we were able to boil about a litre of milk, though it took quite some time – more than fifteen minutes, I think. We were not provided evening tea in prison; but thanks to the Red Cross, for about a month we were able to enjoy the comfort of a hot glass of milk or a glass of tea in the evening. We hoped the Red Cross would remember us again, but they did not.

The other visit was not so pleasant. It was that of an Italian journalist, one Emile Marini. The man, as we learnt later, was an unscrupulous mercenary, and had been commissioned by the Portuguese government to write and publish in European newspapers favourable reports about the situation in Goa[1] which had made news all over the world since the launching of the freedom movement in August, 1954. The gist of Portuguese propaganda in those days was that all Goans lived in perfect happiness under Portuguese rule, that there was no freedom movement as such in Goa, and that whatever "disturbances of peace" that occurred there, were the work of "Indian" agents. Signor Marini was now engaged to play second fiddle to this tune. He came to Goa as an honoured guest of the Portuguese government and viewed things from angles indicated to him by his hosts. One of the items in Signor Marini's guided viewing programme was taking a look at political prisoners. Accordingly, the Italian reporter came to Altinho prison accompanied by a few police officers. I think, the police authorities had intended to show Signor Marini only non-Goan Indian prisoners at Altinho; for the existence of hundreds of Goan prisoners would not have fitted in with the narrow, angular view of things which he was expected to take. Perhaps it was by mistake then, that he was brought to some of the cells occupied by Goan prisoners, or perhaps the authorities did not mind showing some of us, trusting that the Italian would not allow his awareness of our existence to disturb his perspective.

Anyhow, ours was one of the cells which was opened to him. When he began to question us we said we wished to know whom we had the honour of speaking to; and he introduced himself. Speaking in English, in which he was quite fluent, he asked us why we were in prison. I, being a little more fluent in the language than others in our cell, answered on behalf of all: "That is a question," I said, "perhaps not to be addressed to us, as we feel, we have not committed any crime to merit imprisonment."

---

1. [On his return to Europe. Emile Marini wrote and published in Portugal the book *Goa, Tal Como a Vi* (Goa As I Saw It) giving his cock-eyed impressions of Goa].

"But people are not just arrested for nothing," he said.

"Here in Goa people are arrested for doing and saying things which, in Italy for instance, are considered the legitimate rights of people." I replied.

He snorted and then asked, "What exactly did you do?"

I then patiently related to him that we were all members of a patriotic non-violent organisation of Goans and that all we had done was to demonstrate our desire for freedom from Portuguese rule.

"But what is wrong with the Portuguese?" he asked.

"Nothing is wrong with them so long as they remain in their own country." I said. "What we don't want is foreign rule. I suppose you would not like your Italy to be ruled by the Americans even if the Americans turn out to be the best of rulers." He snorted again.

"You say you don't want Portuguese rule, but most of the people outside are happy with Portuguese rule." he added.

"How do you know?" I asked. "Let the people be assured complete freedom of expression and then you will know what they think about Portuguese rule." He gave a final snort and then withdrew with a stiff nod.

Among the police officers accompanying the Italian journalist, only one, a Goan, knew English, and I had observed him following our discussion with a frown on his face. The European officers not knowing English had at first shrugged their shoulders at the incomprehensible talk, and then spent the time idly looking down at their boots. On their departure, all of us in the cell exchanged excited impressions about the interview. However, after the initial elation at having scored off against the Italian pressman, we began to consider in all sobriety the consequences to me of my talking so freely with the journalist. It was to be expected that the police authorities would take a serious view of the "offence" and would mete out some "punishment." I thought that I might be taken out and beaten and then put into solitary confinement. There had been cases before of prisoners who having given offence to the authorities in some way or the other were kept in solitary confinement for long periods of even three and four months. I now prepared myself mentally to go through that punishment.

A prisoner put into solitary confinement was deprived of all human company. In the morning he was taken out separately when all the other prisoners were put back in their cells. The hotel boys who brought our food[2] were not allowed to see him, but were ordered to keep the food-plate outside at the door, and then the prisoner was made to take it himself. He was not allowed any reading material. Sometimes he was not allowed visits. And he was harassed in many little ways. The only people he saw thrice a day were the same prison guards who usually acted surly and hardly spoke to him. Some prisoners put into solitary confinement for long periods could not bear the inactivity and the loneliness within four walls to which they were condemned, and they emerged from it greatly broken in spirit. There was at least one case of a prisoner suffering a mental break-down after going through solitary confinement for a number of months. In his case other factors might have also contributed to the breakdown, but solitary confinement, was, I believe the decisive factor. I suppose man needs both activity and human company for his mental sanity – meaningful activity, more perhaps, than the company of his fellows. And prisoners in normal circumstances would not only get the company of other prisoners but would also keep themselves busy by together improvising games to play or other things to do. But a prisoner shut up alone in a small cell and having nothing to do, but day in and day out, stare at the four walls and brood over dark thoughts, was in ideal conditions to go mad.

However, when the police guards did not come to take me away either that evening or the next day, we began to surmise that the Goan police officer had perhaps not reported to the higher police authorities my talk with the Italian journalist and that our fears about my "punishment" were unfounded. And that is how it proved to be. But so much had I prepared myself to go through the ordeal

---

2. [A certain hotel supplied food on contract, to prisoners at police headquarters and at Altinho Prison. At Aguada Fort and at Reis Magos Fort prisoners had the facility of cooking their own food]

that the realization that I had escaped solitary confinement, in fact, brought me a little regret. I do not know how far I would have withstood the ordeal, but at that time I felt that I had missed a great experience – a trial which would have tested my powers of endurance. Undoubtedly, even ordinary imprisonment is a test of one's mettle, but solitary imprisonment would be a supreme test, I thought. The enforced loneliness together with all the constricting restraints placed upon him would deprive a person of all the satisfactions which he normally derives from his surroundings. He would be thrown entirely on his own inner resources for his mental well-being. It would be a challenge to his spirit – a challenge which might call forth his latent powers of endurance. And he might come through the experience greatly transformed. But fate did not have in store for me that great experience.

23

TRANSFER TO AGUADA FORT PRISON

After spending about seven months at Altinho Prison we began to hear of rumours that all the prisoners at Altinho would be transferred to Aguada Fort prison. Probably the information was given by some prison guards to some of the prisoners. We heard that the cells at police headquarters were again getting full; and so we were to be moved to Aguada Fort to make room at Altinho for the prisoners from police headquarters. These rumours acted on prisoners' spirits like balm on raw sores. In the hard and dreary conditions of prison life, any little change which promised to be an improvement in our life was looked forward to by all prisoners with great expectations. And this promised to be a great change. Conditions had been really bad at Altinho, and we had heard that in comparison they were much better at Aguada. For one thing, prisoners there were allowed to cook their own food, and that in itself would be a great blessing; for another, the military were in charge of the prison, and soldiers do not have the reputation of being mean and nasty as the police have.

Then suddenly, about a week after we had heard the first rumours, we were told at the time of the evening meal, by the police corporal on duty to get ready early the next morning to move to Aguada Fort. That same evening, with great joy we packed our few personal belongings in tin boxes or cloth bags, and then went to sleep with a light heart. About four o'clock in the morning, after a hurried wash we were asked to file in the corridor with all our things. And immediately after, we were ushered into closed vans, and while the whole city of Panjim was still fast asleep, we were transported through its deserted streets to the jetty of Panjim-Betim ferry, where a launch was waiting to take us to Aguada Fort, down at the mouth of the river Mandovi. We were all herded into the hold of the launch, while on its deck a number of police guards armed with sten-guns took their positions. The launch then chugged down the river and at first light reached the jetty below Fort Aguada.

I had seen the Fort many years before, as a young boy, but it was from a distance (people generally were stopped at an outer wall, far from the gate of the fort), and I had not been much impressed. Now from the river below, and at close quarters, it had a monstrous and sinister aspect. It looked all the more sinister to us because we were entering it as prisoners. As we were being taken in by the main gate, we noted that the high massive wall towering menacingly above us seemed to dwarf us, reducing all human figures to insignificance. I had the feeling of being taken as a captive in some frightful medieval castle, and I wondered how much of my youthful life I would have to spend immured within those cruel walls. But the terrifying impression that the fort produced on us was more the effect of its huge, intimidating walls; for once inside, having a view of the neat, harmless looking whitewashed prison-houses constructed within the fort, we felt more at ease.

Aguada Fort is situated on the rocky promontory at the mouth of the river Mandovi. Built in the early seventeenth century on the orders of one of the kings of the Spanish dynasty that for some time ruled the combined kingdom of Spain and Portugal, the fort had played an important role in the defence of Goa in the age of Portuguese-Dutch colonial rivalry. There used to be a large military garrison stationed here then; and its cannon, mounted along the riverside wall, had guarded the fluvial approach to the capital of Goa. Now, those guns, relics of a past age, were ranged along the outer wall by the river, together with a heap of cannon-balls near each gun – all serving an ornamental purpose.

When the period of colonial rivarly had drawn to a close, the fort had lost much of its military importance, and then with the passage of time it had come to be increasingly utilised as a prison. A small garrison, however had always been stationed there, its soldiers serving the purpose of guarding the prisoners. Those involved in revolts against the government in the nineteenth and the early twentieth centuries had been imprisoned in Aguada Fort. And coming to recent times, most of those who had taken a leading part in the 1946 movement had also been incarcerated here. In fact, in the days of the freedom struggle, for most Goans, Aguada Fort was identical with "Prison". It was the fort's long use as a prison, coupled perhaps with its forbidding appearance, that had given it the reputation of a *Bastille* almost, among the Goan people.

Since the beginning of the freedom movement of 1954, the fort was used as a prison exclusively for political offenders. Before we were brought here, there were already about thirty prisoners, and with our arrival the number went up to over three hundred.

As more and more troops were brought to Goa since the beginning of the freedom movement, the strength of the garrison at the fort had also been increased. At the time of our arrival at Aguada there must have been between two to three hundred soldiers stationed at the fort. But the soldiers' quarters (including the Commandant's) were not actually in the fort, but just outside, the buildings inside the fort being all utilised as prisons.

On our arrival the Commandant of Fort Aguada, Captain Costa-Afonso, a man as proud as Punch about his military calling, came to see us and to supervise our installation in the different prisons cells. There were eight large cells at Aguada, some large enough to accommodate more than fifty prisoners. I was put in a cell containing about fifty prisoners, most of us arrivals from Altinho, and a few Aguada old-timers, who gave us a hearty welcome, and helped us to settle in the place. The comforts of these Aguada cells were a very pleasant change as they were in sharp constrast to the hardships we had borne at Altinho and at police headquarters. The most satisfying features of these cells were that each of them was provided with a kitchen, and each had a bathroom and a toilet attached to it. The facility to cook our own food not only resulted in our having better food than in our previous prisons, but it also made us feel a great sense of freedom. And the bathroom and toilet within the cell were a great relief from an anxiety which only prisoners can understand – prisoners who have had to depend on the whim of the prison guard to be taken out to answer the call of nature.

The old prisoners who were here before us had been brought to Aguada before the beginning of 1955. Most of them were patriots of great renown, being connected with important events in the history of the freedom movement. Among these were members of the first Working Committee of N.C.(G) in Goa, whose arrest in June 1954, before the movement was officially launched in August, 1954, had made great news in Goa.[1] Then there were some of those who had participated in the famous "March on Goa" on 15th August, 1954,[2] an event which had launched the movement and which being widely publicised in the international press, had focussed the world's attention on "the problem of Goa." We felt it was a matter of great fortune for us youngsters to live in prison with all these veterans of the freedom movement, some of them men of great experience and knowledge. And for these old prisoners who had spent an uneventful year here in comparative loneliness, our arrival was a matter of great rejoicing. Their number was considerable, yet having no clear idea of the development of the freedom struggle outside, there being hardly any new prisoners brought to Aguada for about a year, they had felt keenly their isolation from the world. Now the arrival of a large mass of prisoners was to them a clear testimony that the freedom movement, which they had helped to launch, was still expanding.

---

1. [Among those were Advocate Pandurang Mulgaonkar, Doctor J.F. Martins, Advocate Gop l Appa Kamat, Mr. Shankar Dessai and others.]

2. [Most of the 15th August prisoners were. in the beginning kept at Reis Magos fort Prison and only later brought to Aguada. But a few others like Mr. Alfred Afonso. Mr. Ramkrishna Karpe were at Aguada. The other prominent Aguada old timers (arrested before 1955) were Mr. Alvaro Pereira. Mr Nanda Gaitonde. etc.]

24

SETTLING DOWN TO A NEW ROUTINE AT AGUADA

The system of feeding prisoners at Aguada Fort prison was this: Every prisoner was allotted by the government an amount of one rupee five annas per day, and with this amount he was to get all his requirements of food. But no money was given in the hands of the prisoners, nor was each prisoner supposed to prepare his food separately. All the prisoners in a cell together were expected to maintain a collective account, and prepare their food in common, and live within the amount allotted to them. For the management of house-keeping within the cell, the Commandant of the Fort appointed from among the prisoners a "chief of the cell" who would be responsible to him for the proper maintenance of accounts of the entire cell. Every day the chief of the cell submitted to the authorities a requisition of the provisions we needed, and a military jeep went and brought us those provisions. At the end of the month the chief of the cell presented the account of the monthly expenditure of the cell to the Commandant, who checked and approved it. What the Commandant required was that our total expenditure should not exceed the total amount allotted in the month to all the prisoners in the cell.

In those days i.e. in the 1950's when the cost of living was quite low, we could have reasonably good food with the allotment of one rupee five annas per prisoner. If each prisoner was to prepare his food separately, that amount might not have been sufficient for his day's food. But there was an advantage in thirty or forty prisoners pooling their allotments together and preparing their meals in common. In fact, we did not spend the whole amount of one rupee five annas on food alone. Prisoners decided among themselves that a few annas from each one's daily allotment should be set aside for each prisoner's personal expense, like buying tooth-paste, shaving blades, writing paper, etc. It was a principle generally adopted by all prisoners that we should live entirely at the cost of the government, and should not, in any way, be a burden to our family. Hence, as far as possible, we did not ask for anything from home.

We began to settle down here at Aguada prison to a new kind of routine, and a different kind of life from that spent in other prisons. I experienced a feeling of permanence here, a feeling of having reached my final destination as a prisoner, knowing that I would have to spend long years here, till my release in the unforeseeable future. What I could foresee was that our group would soon be brought to trial, and that we would be convicted and awarded long terms of imprisonment. So with a feeling of being already a confirmed convict I began to put my heart into all the activities available to us here. And it was the opportunity for various kinds of activities that gave a sense of satisfaction to our life, and in the long run rendered the monotony of long imprisonment bearable.

The opportunity to cook our own food provided us with exciting activity, particularly in the beginning when it was all new to us. And men who had never entered the kitchen having always considered it as the woman's domain – now began to apply their minds to mastering the culinary art. To begin with, we divided the whole population of the cell into six or seven batches, and drew up a schedule of kitchen duty for these batches. Each batch did the day's cooking in rotation. People who knew a little about cooking assumed the positions of chief cooks in different batches, and the others assisted them in various ways. Everyone, even the elderly and the infirm, helped in some way or the other. Doctors and lawyers, clerks and merchants who might not have known physical labour, now tried to be of service by slicing onions, cutting vegetables, cleaning utensils or tending the fire. The young and the strong took upon themselves the harder tasks of the kitchen, like grinding *masala*. This grinding of *masala* for forty or fifty people – *masala* for curry, *bhaji* and other preparations – had to be done with huge grinding stones and was rather a difficult job. I always liked physical work, and knowing I had no talent for cooking, I volunteered to be a *masala* grinder in our batch. It was mechanical, brainless work – work fit for an ox, someone might say. But it had its own compensation: The rhythmic movements involved in that work stimulated the mind to think, and sometimes left it free to wander as it chose. So much so that the kitchen work that I did at Aguada Prison is always associated in my memory with the pleasant hours of contemplation and daydreaming that I spent at the grinding stone! For some time our inexperienced cooks indulged in experimentation, but gradually they learnt the art and some of them in fact emerged as fine cooks. It was indeed remarkable that with the limited amount of money allotted to us we could have sufficient food, and rather good food. It was all a result of proper planning and good cooking.

When it was one's turn to work in the kitchen once in six or seven days, one was busy throughout the day and usually tired by the end of the day. Besides this, there was the daily work of bringing and storing water for the general use of the cell – for cooking, for washing, and for everyone's bath. We brought this water in kerosene tins (to which we had fixed bamboo handles) from outside the fort, from a large well with a perennial supply, and we stored it in our cell in big tin drums. Every morning we had to make two or three trips to the well accompanied by a couple of armed guards. In this work too, every prisoner was found willing to do his bit – even those unaccustomed to physical work, including the elderly and weak, came staggering under the weight of a heavy tin of water on their head; while the young and strong came panting with two tins in their hands. This work lasted for about thirty minutes and provided us with good morning exercise. Besides that exercise, in accordance with prison regulations, every evening we were taken out in the courtyard in front of the prison house, and allowed to walk up and down for half an hour under the watchful eyes of armed guards stationed at certain points in the courtyard.

25

PORTRAIT OF THE COMMANDANT OF THE FORT

But at the beginning of our life here, in the midst of the general satisfaction, we had one irritation in the person of the Commandant of the fort, Captain Costa-Afonso. He was a regular thorn in our side. From the beginning itself we took a strong dislike to him. He stood erect like a ramrod and barked out orders both at the men under his command and at us prisoners; and he expected us too to stand at ramrod attention before him and carry out his orders with military promptness. The man had a soul of a drill-master; he was an incarnation of the military spirit at its silliest. He was so obsessed with military discipline that, I think, he would have been happy standing stiffly all his life on parade ground shouting military commands. There was no flexibility about the man; he was stiff and rigid both in body and mind; and he always seemed to be in high gear for action. It was clear that if he were to go on living in that style he would soon reach the breaking-point.

Captain Costa-Afonso with his narrow and rigid barrack mentality often had conflicts with prisoners whose life he sought to rule with an iron hand. And he punished those who displeased him by condemning them to spend a number of days in the "Dark Cell". This dark cell was a beastly hole of a room with hardly enough space for a prisoner to lie down. It had no window, only a small door which, when closed, turned the room pitch dark. The Commandant thought that he could break the spirit of the prisoners by shutting them in the Dark Cell for six or seven days; but it turned out that prisoners were not much afraid of that punishment, as that dark-cell confinement was of a short duration.

It was not only the prisoners that he harassed; even his own subordinates – particularly the common soldiers – suffered under his high-handedness. Sometimes we heard some of them grumbling against him or even cursing him behind his back.

But to be fair to the man, it could not be said that the military training he had received had entirely squeezed out his humanity and turned him into an automaton; though that was how I was tempted to judge his character in the beginning. For gradually he began to show the better side of his nature. The first good quality that we observed in him was his love of cleanliness. It was to our advantage; for it was mainly due to his insistence on cleanliness that prisoners lived in proper hygienic conditions. His concern with cleanliness might have been seen as a part of his military mentality. But there were still other ways in which he showed himself humane. Whenever a prisoner happened to be ill he took personal interest in his recovery, coming to see him along with the military compounder, even at night. The government doctor used to visit our prison only once a week. But there were two or three doctors among the prisoners. The Commandant, when he felt it necessary, would call these doctors from different cells to examine a sick prisoner, and to hold a consultation. The way he acted with vigour to stamp out sickness in the fort, it appeared as if he could not tolerate it in his jurisdiction. He also took enough interest in our food. If he happened to visit our cell before meal-time, he would want to know what items of food we had prepared. Removing the lids of our cooking vessels he would peer at the contents, asking detailed questions about each preparation. He would particularly admire our Kokum curry (which is a mere digestive), being intrigued by its wine-red colour, and whenever he had an official visitor to the prison he would make it a point to show him this curry as one of the wonders of the Indian cuisine.

A few months after our arrival there was a change of Commandant, and Captain Costa-Afonso was taken out of Goa and posted to some other Portuguese colony. We did not exactly miss him because the subsequent Commandants proved to be more agreeable, as they did not interfere in the life of prisoners, taking it as their duty only to guard the prison and to supply the prisoners with provisions within the allotted amount of money. But a few years later when we learnt that Captain Costa Afonso had died in an air crash in Angola (the Angolan war of independence was at its height then), I felt sorry for the man whose life at one point had crossed our life, and whom tragic death had now placed beyond the pale of enmity.

26

INTELLECTUAL PURSUITS AND CREATIVE DIVERSIONS AMONG PRISONERS

Save for the kitchen work once a week and the daily fetching of water, we were free most of the day, six days in the week. But hardly any prisoner spent his time in idleness. The kind of conditions we lived in here at Aguada provided prisoners with opportunities to pursue some activity or the other of their liking. Almost every prisoner desired to broaden his mind by means of reading newspapers, magazines and books, all of which were now available to us in sufficient numbers. Indian newspapers were, of course, banned in Goa at that time; but we used to receive Goan newspapers in Portuguese and Pakistani papers in English, which provided news about Goa and the Indian sub-continent. All these papers were biased no doubt, but it was better than getting no news at all. For international news we used to depend on foreign papers and magazines like, *The Manchester Guardian*, *The New Statesman*, *Time* and *Newsweek* which were regularly sent to us by some kind friends and relatives of some of the prisoners.

Then we had books, mostly in English, but some also in Portuguese, Marathi and Hindi. Some of the prisoners who could afford, used to get their own books; and besides, we used to borrow many books from the non-Goan Indian prisoners (now also brought to Aguada), who used to receive their regular supply of books through the Egyptian consul. These prisoners were kept in two separate small cells which had no cooking facilities, and hence we used to provide food to one of these cells. Two or three of us would go to that cell with the food accompanied by a guard who after opening the door would usually remain outside. While returning we would take books from the non-Goan prisoners, and covering them with some wrapping paper we would slip them into the empty food vessels, and thus smuggle them into our cell. With our own books and the borrowed ones (most of which we did not return), we built our little library, placing the books on little shelves neatly arranged in different sections according to language and subject. In the course of about three years we had collected a few hundred books. And many of us made good use of this library.

Apart from reading newspapers and books for pleasure and information, a number of prisoners now engaged themselves in serious intellectual pursuits. Some undertook the study of languages, while others sought knowledge of subjects like psychology and philosophy with the help of whatever books we had in our library, and under the guidance of men well-versed in the subjects. With so many prisoners reading, studying, and discussing intellectual matters, a sort of academic atmosphere was created in our prison cell, which induced even the weak-willed to make some effort aimed at self-improvement.

I had always been fond of reading, and I could have spent all my time only reading different books for pleasure. But with a little effort of the will I set myself to study two languages – Hindi and French – which I had not learnt at school. I was fortunate to have in our cell persons who could teach me these languages systematically. In about two years' time I had the great satisfaction of knowing Hindi well enough to speak it fluently, to write it reasonably well, and to read, and appreciate some of the works of Premchand and Rahul Sankrutayan which we had in our prison library. As for French, my progress in this language was rather slow for want of books; yet it was sufficient to enable me to take French as my second language when I joined college after my release. In fact, my study of both these languages proved to be provident, as I needed them for the prosecution of my college studies.[1]

Another regular activity in our cell was the "cultural programme" that we used to have on a fixed day every week. It usually consisted of a talk given by a prisoner on some topic of general interest, followed by discussion of the same. It was mostly men of learning – doctors, lawyers, teachers – who gave the talks, enlightening us

1. [I have a life long indebtedness to Advocate Pandurang Mulgaonkar for teaching me French, and to the late Mr. Januario Pereira for teaching me Hindi.]

youngsters on so many matters. Sometimes the talks and discussions would be on current events of world significance about which we felt strongly. In fact, during the period of three and a half years I spent at Aguada prison, a number of electrifying, world-shaking events occurred in different parts of the world.

There was the nationalisation of the Suez Canal by Egypt and its serious sequels: the invasion and occupation of the Canal Zone by a confederation of Anglo-French forces; then the threat of massive intervention by the Soviet Union, which in turn raised the frightful spectre of another World War. But in this situation it was interesting, and also encouraging, for us to read that in the Security Council of the United Nations both the U.S.A. and the U.S.S.R. had for the first time voted together on the same side, condemning the Anglo-French military action and urging an immediate pull-out of their forces. This joint voting by the super powers raised great hopes for an understanding between them, and for their co-operation in preserving peace in the world. I remember how we followed with keen interest all those developments of the Suez Canal question and what animated discussions we had on every turn of the event.

Then there was the thrilling event of the launching of the first artificial satellite, *Sputnik*, by the Soviet Union – an event hailed by the world press as a turning point in the history of mankind. Even in the dismal conditions of prison life we felt elated, contemplating the prospects that this event opened up for mankind. I was particularly reminded of H.G. Wells's prophetic words in *The Outline of History* that "Life,.. under the leadership of man ... would presently stand upon Earth, as upon a footstool, and spread its realms amidst the stars." Well, here was man standing poised to spread his "realms amidst the stars". But was he worthy to undertake that glorious mission when there were all kinds of dissensions among mankind, when there was so much oppression on this earth – an oppression epitomized by our incarceration in Aguada Fort?

I also remember the great excitement with which we read in '*The New Statesman*,' the open letter addressed by the English philosopher, Bertrand Russel to the President of the United States (Eisenhower), and the Secretary of the Communist Party of the U.S.S.R. (Krushchev). Bertrand Russel feared that the arms race between the super powers might culminate in a nuclear holocaust – a holocaust that might annihilate the human race. And in his letter to the leaders of the rival power blocks he made an impassioned plea that they renounce the use of force in the settlement of international disputes, and that they help to free mankind from the curse of nuclear weapons. Krushchev and Foster Dulles (American Secretary of State) answered that letter stating and trying to justify the positions of their respective countries on the questions of disarmament and nuclear weapons. Finally, the *New Statesman* brought Bertrand Russel's second letter chiding the two leaders for their fanaticism, but at the same time, pointing out certain areas of agreement in their positions. We had felt at that time that though the correspondence initiated by Bertrand Russel might not directly lead to disarmament, yet it would make people all over the world aware of the threat posed by nuclear weapons to the very survival of the human race.

All such exciting reports that we read in the foreign papers about great world events deeply stirred our minds and set us pondering over, and discussing those events for weeks together. Most of us were young idealists, and our involvement in a cause like the freedom of Goa had reinforced our idealism which now grew and encompassed the whole world. Though we were only helpless prisoners in a remote corner of the world, I considered our concern about those great events whose course would shape tomorrow's world, to be a legitimate and worthy concern, reflecting, as it did, our hopes and aspirations for a better world; and I felt it in my heart that such hopes and aspirations of even the mute sections of mankind would somehow avail in the long run.

Apart from all those intellectual activities, there were available to prisoners other diversions which provided outlets for various talents and skills. Some prisoners tried their hands at tailoring, stitching clothes for daily wear, for themselves and others. A few of these finally could stitch suitable shirts and pants, all without the use of the sewing machine. The cloth they generally used was empty flour bags (flour in cloth bags was then imported from abroad) which were available quite cheap, but which yielded good, strong cloth. There was one prisoner who, after some practice, became an adept in the feminine arts of sewing, embroidery and knitting. He appeared to be the last person in whom one could expect those feminine graces, being sturdily built with a thick, dark, masculine moustache; and he had hands which seemed to have been fashioned by nature to wield tools like crow-bars, sledge-hammers and pick-axes. It was a real wonder to see those powerful, muscular hands nimbly plying various types of needles. And the products of his craft – knitted sweaters, embroidered pillow cases and kerchiefs, etc. – were real marvels.

A few prisoners tried to do a little of carpentry with some simple tools which were allowed in prison. They took hold of pinewood boxes in which we used to receive some provisions, and they made beautiful shelves for our library from pinewood planks. They also made other little things of wood for various uses.

The prison authorities had made no provision for a barber at Aguada prison – somehow, they seemed to have overlooked the prisoners' need to have their hair cut. But, in fact, we never felt the need of a barber, as many youngsters were eager to try their hand at this craft too. Again, in the beginning, it was all experimentation with varied results: some rather satisfactory, some quite funny, some even a little painful. However, in the course of a few months we had a number of competent hair dressers who were much in demand.

Like other youngsters I also was fascinated by the idea of acquiring some manual skills; and the first craft that I tried to learn was that of a barber. With great difficulty I persuaded a young prisoner to sit for a hair-cut, and then I set to work with some measure of self-confidence and a great deal of enthusiasm. But as I proceeded I realised that the work was not so easy. And finally the attempt ended in a dismal failure. My hair-dressing art only succeeded in giving an appearance of a misshapen head to my victim; and the poor fellow remained an object of fun for weeks, until his hair grew enough and another hair-cut by a more skilled hair dresser restored the natural shape of his head. Still, after my failure, I wanted to persist in learning the craft. But my first performance had already established my reputation as a hopeless barber, and no one was willing to stake his hair and consequently his appearance to my hair-cutting skills.

The other craft at which I tried my hand was sewing. My intention was to stitch myself the clothes that I needed while I remained in jail – shirts and shorts for daily wear. I ordered some empty flour bags, and after washing them got the cloth cut for a shirt by someone who had mastered the art of cutting (as it was something which I could never manage). Then I patiently stitched the cut parts together, producing a garment which somewhat resembled a shirt. But it served its purpose – somehow I could wriggle into it, and it kept me warm in the cold and the rainy seasons. Later I stitched other items of clothing; and as long as I was in jail I never asked for any clothes from home.

27

OUR TRIAL

I am Sentenced to Twelve Years of Imprisonment

About two months after our transfer to Aguada, every member of our group was served with a charge-sheet issued by the Portuguese Military Tribunal in Goa. In this document the State Prosecutor accused us in substance, of having belonged to, and worked for the National Congress (Goa), a subversive organization which sought to overthrow Portuguese sovereignty in Goa – a crime punishable under such and such sections of the Portuguese Penal Code. Against me, in addition to the above, there was the specific charge of having enlisted a number of people into the conspiracy to overthrow Portuguese rule – again a crime punishable under some other section of the said code. The charge-sheet also mentioned that if we so desired we could opt for our own defence lawyer, in which case the Military Court had to be informed within a certain period, or else we would be defended by the State Attorney, some army officer attached to the Military Court.

Of course there was no point in engaging a private lawyer for our defence, as we did not desire to deny the "crimes" of which we were accused, and to get out of the clutches of the Portuguese law. What we stood for was rejection of the whole Portuguese regime together with its laws; and hence, we felt, taking cognizance of their laws and defending ourselves in their framework would be tantamount to acceptance of their laws. It was usually prisoners arrested on suspicion, and eager to get out of jail, that engaged the services of private lawyers.[1]

But it was interesting to speculate how the Military Court

pleader would defend us. He was a mere legal formality, and in our case an irrelevant formality, as we all meant to stand by all our actions against Portuguese rule; and we needed none of his defence. Yet we were eagerly looking forward to seeing how the gentleman would play his paradoxical role!

Then about a month after being served with the charge-sheets we were produced in the Military Court for trial. There were altogether thirteen members of our original group who had been arrested and were now brought to trial. (By the time of our arrest the strength of our group had been about twenty-five. But all had not been arrested. Some had evaded arrest at that time, but had later offered *satyagraha* along with other groups of N.C.(G) workers, and so were tried separately with those groups. A few escaped from Goa and for years lived outside). Along with our group a smaller group from Mapusa area was also tried. These two groups were tried together because some of the activities of our group were connected with the activities of the other group. So that in all, there were about eighteen of us tried together.[2]

---

1. [The situation faced in court by non-violent prisoners in Goa was basically different from that faced by non-violent prisoners in British India. First of all, all freedom fighters in Goa were tried by the military court, whereas in British India it was the civil courts that tried all civilian freedom fighters. More important still, the British never denied the principle of self-rule to the Indian people; and hence it was possible for freedom fighters to defend themselves in the court in the context of British laws. But Salazar's government, by a stroke of the pen, had transformed overnight all Portuguese colonies into "integral parts of the Portuguese Nation," and consequently seeking independence for any of the colonies, was, in the view of Portuguese law, an act of treason punishable by long years of rigorous imprisonment. And once you stood for freedom, you faced the full hostility of the law, and there was no question of defence.]

2. [The following were the members of our group who were tried and sentenced: our teachers Mr. Pereira, Mr. Pinto and Mr. Godinho, all from Aldona; Jerry Pinto (Aldona), Inacinho D'Souza (Aldona), Pascoal Rocha (Aldona), Bonifacio Nunes (Chórao), Henry D'Souza (Tivim), Calista Araujo (Siolim), Mitra Kakodkar (Siolim), Joaquim Pinto (Assonora), Rafael D'Souza (Assonora) and myself. The other group consisted of Dr. Dubhashi (Mapusa), Mahableshwar Naik (Mapusa), Sridhar Sirsat (Parra) and others].

We were tried by a panel of three judges, two of them military officers of high rank, and the third a judge from the civil court, who acted as the presiding judge. The three judges sat together at a long raised table. On either side of the judges, and a little in front, sat the State Prosecutor and the Court lawyer also at raised tables. All these military officers were elegantly dressed in immaculate white uniforms on which dazzled their epaulettes and decorations. The two military judges also wore ceremonial swords. A little away from the court lawyer sat the private lawyer Mr. Tamba, who was to defend one or two members of the Mapusa group. In front of the judges at a low table sat the court clerk and interpreter, a military officer of lower rank. Behind the court clerk we prisoners sat on benches in two rows, facing the judges. Immediately behind us was some kind of a railing and behind this railing sat a squad of soldiers armed with bayoneted rifles.

In the midst of the military officers sat the civil judge Mr. Quadros, a Goan who had gained notoriety among prisoners for his hatred of freedom fighters. He had presided over dozens of such trials, and had meted out harsh sentences to hundreds of freedom fighters. He was dressed in a dark suit, and the way he perched on his high seat, and bent his head on either side to talk to the military officers, it brought to my mind the image of the vulture, and this image of the vulture persisted in my mind till the end of the trial. Naturally, in the eyes of all Goan patriots, Mr. Quadros was a repulsive figure because of the brazen and shameless way in which he collaborated with the Portuguese regime in this nefarious work of persecuting nationalists. In the court itself he stood out, the only Goan civilian among the Portuguese military officers – a traitor to his own people. [3]

The court assembled at ten o'clock in the morning and took up the work of examining the charges against each prisoner. One by one we were called up in front of the judge and asked a few questions concerning the "crimes" of which we were accused. It was always a

---

3. [About two months after our trial, Mr. Quadros's collaborations with the Portuguese regime had a setback. Some nationalist sent him by post a parcel-bomb, which on being opened exploded and blew off most of the fingers of his right hand, and also disfigured his face and permanently impaired his hearing. It was said that he had narrowly escaped death.]

part of the philosophy of National Congress (Goa), part of the philosophy of non-violence that one can serve the cause of freedom by remaining in jail. Hence when I was taken forward and questioned I admitted everything that was recorded in my police report, and took upon myself the major responsibility of having organized our group. In fact everyone admitted all the charges against him. After completing this work the court adjourned for the afternoon.

When it reassembled at four o'clock, the presiding judge opened the proceedings by inviting the State Prosecutor to address the court. That worthy military gentleman in a long rambling speech tried to prove how all our actions constituted serious crimes against Portuguese sovereignty. He argued that our crimes merited severe punishment because our conspiracy against the state was coolly planned for so many months, and because he did not find any extenuating circumstances in our guilt. He singled out certain people and demanded that the maximum penalty provided by law be meted out to them: the three teachers of our group, and the doctor from the Mapusa group, for being in the conspiracy against the state with all their maturity and education; and he named me too for having "instigated" so many people to act against Portuguese sovereignty. I was quite pleased that the State Prosecutor had included my name in his demand for maximum punishment, because I realised that I was greatly responsible for many of my companions' participation in the freedom struggle, and I did not want to shirk bearing the consequences of that responsibility.

Then the state counsel for defence addressed the Court. He did not even make a pretence of defending us, but pleaded that the honourable Military Court should take a serious view of our crimes against Portuguese sovereignty. In fact his speech did not differ in substance from the Prosecutor's speech. But I had the impression that the gentleman was uncomfortable in his position of counsel for defence, being aware of his paradoxical and irrelevant role.

Then it was the turn of the private lawyer Mr. Tamba to address the court. I had been thinking that a private defence counsel would be ineffectual in a court like this. But advocate Tamba took us all by surprise: he put up a very fine performance. Knowing that he could not defend his clients (who were genuine patriots), in the framework of Portuguese laws, he launched on a bold and vigorous tirade on the injustice and harshness of these laws, which made the military judges alternately wince and frown. And he was a far better orator than the military officers, being in command of a more elegant and more refined language. From his unusual performance in the court it was obvious to us all, as it must have been obvious to the military officers in the court, that Advocate Tamba was a fearless patriot. Now the question that rose in our minds was: how long he would be left free to go on attacking Portuguese laws. Though his positon gave him some immunity to function as he did, I could very well envisage the possibility of the government authorities getting the police to arrest him, even on trumped-up charges.[4]

By the time the private defence lawyer finished his address it was about six o'clock in the evening, and the court adjourned again. We thought that it had finished its business for the day, and that we would be brought again some other day to hear the verdicts. But we were taken to an adjoining room and left sitting there, under guard. A little later Advocate Tamba informed us that the court wanted to complete our trial that day itself, even if they had to work till midnight and that the judges, after some refreshment, would retire to an inner chamber to decide our fate.

It took them quite a long time to decide on the sentences and to get them typed. When the court finally reassmbled for the last and most important act of the trial, it was past ten o'clock in the night. All the noises of the city which we had been hearing throughout the day had by now ceased, and the lights in all the buildings were out. The silence and stillness of the surrounding city amidst which the Military Court assembled lent greater solemnity to the closing part of its proceedings. After the judges and counsels had taken their places, and the presiding judge had made a few remarks, the sergeant in command of the squad of soldiers brought them to attention and then ordered them to present arms. At the same time the two military judges stood at attention and drawing out their swords presented them. The shouting of commands, the rattling of rifles, the flashing of bayonets and swords, were all most impressive in their effect. The Military Court at this final juncture presented a fine spec-

---

4. [What I had envisaged came to pass in due course. A few months after our trial we learnt from a new prisoner of Advocate Tamba's arrest. And some time later he himself came to join us at Aguada in our very cell, in fact. He took to prison life quite cheerfully, declaring that he had foreseen prison as his inevitable destiny once he had decided to be outspoken in the military court.]

tacle – we thought it was all in our honour, whatever the court might have thought about it.

Then one of the military judges read the sentences in a sonorous voice, as we prisoners listened with rapt attention. Many of my companions were awarded from two to eight years of rigorous imprisonment. And then I heard the judge read out my name: after saying that I had been found guilty of such and such crimes, he read the sentence: ten years of rigorous imprisonment, plus a fine of a large amount, or in lieu of that, another two years of imprisonment – twelve years in all. It was the maximum sentence in our group; and the only other prisoner awarded an equal number of years at this trial was Doctor Dubhashi of the Mapusa group.

The trial ended a little before midnight. While the verdicts of the court were being read I had wondered how our companions would react to their sentences, whether any one would be crushed by his heavy sentence. But now, as we were being driven in a Black Maria through the silent, sleeping city, and across the river, back to our prison-home, Aguada Fort, I was glad to see that everyone was in cheerful spirits. That was a great consolation, as any prisoner repining at his sentence would have greatly demoralised the others. Now, on the contrary, their cheerful acceptance of their sentences showed them to be unwavering, dedicated patriots.

28

PROSPECTS AFTER TRIAL

We had not been dismayed at the long terms of imprisonment pronounced against us because our morale then was quite high. While joining the freedom struggle, we had come prepared for sacrifices, including, of course, the possible sacrifice of the best years of our youthful life. Also, the struggle and the hard days of early prison life we had gone through, had tempered our spirits and further strengthened our resolve to carry the struggle to its conclusion. And finally, while the freedom movement was alive outside, we did not think much of our long sentences, as the continuance of the movement held out the hope of an early collapse of the Portuguese rule.

Still, I cannot say that we were never daunted at all by the prospect of spending twelve, ten or eight precious years of our youthful life in jail. It is easier to act with courage on the impulse of the moment; but the readiness to sit in jail for years without feeling regret at the passing of one's youth, is an attitude most difficult to achieve. This regret was perhaps lurking at the back of the mind, being held in check by our determination to serve the cause of freedom till the end, and by our hope in the ultimate triumph of that cause; but with the passing of years, when the freedom movement seemed to wane, it tried to come up gnawing at, and eroding, that determination and that hope. But most of the prisoners successfully resisted that rising regret and frustration, keeping themselves physically and mentally occupied, taking interest in every activity that prison life afforded.

After the trial, we settled down to the routine of prison life as confirmed convicts. Life at Aguada was everyday mostly the same unvarying life, over and over again. By sheer force of habit one got up in the morning at the usual hour but without anything more eventful to look forward to in the course of the day than the morning breakfast, then lunch, and then supper. As these uneventful days accumulated to months and the months added up to years one could feel a certain weariness creeping over one's spirit. One had to fight off that weariness lest it overwhelmed one's spirit, and turned one's life into a wreck.

In prison, routine is the bane of life, and complete submission to jail routine would have made our life dull and mechanical, killing in us all spontaneity and sensitivity. In the face of the monotony and drift of that life, the great challenge for us was to live with a sense of novelty and freshness, and with a sense of purpose. We seized upon every non-routine activity like reading an interesting book, discussing and savouring some incident, meeting and talking to a new prisoner, to break the monotony of routine life; and despite the severe restraints of prison life, we tried to do a little planning and set ourselves certain goals (like learning a language within a certain time), so that life may not be bereft of purpose. The whole idea was not to allow ourselves to sink into mental apathy, but to retain through the years of prison life our alertness of mind, our sense of humour – in short our mental sanity.

Thus fighting off the frustration and weariness of prison life, we lived from year to year. The procession of changing seasons, which brought pleasant alterations in people's normal life outside, here did little to relieve the monotony of our prison life. All the same, within the limits set by prison conditions, we tried to savour whatever little change the seasons offered us. In summer, in the crowded cells, we suffered from the sultry weather, particularly at night when the breeze dropped and the sea only radiated warmth. But also in summer, due to shortage of water, we were sometimes taken for bath to the river below the fort, where we had the pleasure of diving and collecting mussels from the river-bed. The rainy season, though it brought us relief from the heat, appeared to be a dismal season, as it seemed to accentuate our isolation from the world, surrounding us in gloom. No ships appeared on the sea, no boats on the river. Throughout the season we heard the wind howling outside as the fort stood exposed to the full fury of the gales from the open sea. In that part of the sea visible to us, we would see the foaming breakers advancing towards the fort; and now and then a mighty wave would strike the rampart of the fort with the booming sound of a cannon, setting all the prison buildings vibrating, and sending sea-spray across the courtyard, and through the windows right into our cells.

When I try to recall to mind chronologically the three and half years I spent at Aguada, when I try to remember what all I experienced in the course of that period, I find that I can only visualise the whole duration of my imprisonment as a long, hard journey through a dreary desert – a desert which for vast stretches lay quite featureless, but which fortunately was also dotted at intervals with oasis-like landmarks that made the long journey endurable. These landmarks were some memorable incidents that now and then occurred in the otherwise uneventful months and years of that long period – incidents which relieved the tedium of prison life.

29

A MILITARY CHAPLAIN PREACHES A POLITICAL SERMON

One day, soon after our trial, we were informed by the corporal on duty that a military chaplain would come to conduct mass from the next Sunday at the fort chapel, and that those prisoners who wished to, could attend the religious service. There is a chapel within the Aguada Fort, existing in the same primitive conditions as it must have been when it was built centuries ago – with its rude stone altar, its bare unplastered walls, and its floor paved with flag-stones. On entering it, one is wafted into the past by the sight of the smooth flag-stones worn out over the centuries by the feet of soldiers and perhaps prisoners too.

No Sunday service had been conducted in this chapel since our arrival here, nor did we have those services till the end of our stay at Aguada. I do not know what the arrangement was about the religious needs of the garrison at Aguada, but obviously there was no permanent chaplain attached to the garrison. Perhaps in the absence of a regular chaplain the soldiers were expected to hear mass at one of the neighbouring village churches. This particular chaplain, whose arrival was announced to us, went on saying Sunday mass at the fort chapel for a few months, and then vanished.

Anyhow, many of the prisoners were glad at the opportunity to attend the Sunday mass, and the following Sunday morning a large number of prisoners, Christians and some Hindus too, went to the chapel accompanied by some guards. The chaplain, a man past middle age, holding the rank of lieutenant, welcomed us with a smile and greeted us with kind words. There were some young soldiers attending the mass, but we prisoners made the bulk of his congregation. We were pleased with the man – he really seemed to be kind and fatherly. But the chaplain inspite of his good intentions created a problem for us when he preached his sermon – it was a political harangue, pointedly directed at us prisoners, and holding us up in a bad light.

The theme of his sermon was the spread of Satan's empire in the form of the Communist block, and the event which occasioned the preaching of that sermon was the visit to India of the Russian leaders, Bulganin and Krushchev. It was the first visit of such prominent Soviet leaders to India, and the chaplain saw a terrible calamity in that visit. He firmly believed that the Communist leaders were coming with the collusion of the Indian leader Nehru to clamp and seal the iron curtain over India. What alarmed him was not so much that India was being swallowed by the Communist Camp, but that Satan's empire was reaching right up to the door-step of God-fearing Portuguese Goa. In his sermon the chaplain roundly declared that Nehru had so long been deceiving the world, but that now he stood revealed in his true colours, as the willing accomplice of Communism. And we prisoners also came in for our share of blame. By attempting to integrate Goa into India, we were also becoming the unwitting tools of Communism: we were inviting Satan's rule right into Goa.

This military chaplain with his narrow mental outlook exemplified the tendency found in many Portuguese people to over-simplify inherently complex issues, the tendency to see everything in black and white ignoring all other shades, to divide people into two exclusive classes of angels and devils. Some of us were simply amused at the chaplain's notions; but some were a little agitated: they argued that it would be unpleasant and intolerable if every Sunday when they attended mass they had to hear, instead of a religious sermon, a political harangue condemning India and censuring Goan patriots.

Finally we decided that a few of us should meet the chaplain in a delegation before the next Sunday to let him know that he had hurt our feelings by the kind of preaching he had done, and further to request him to confine himself to religion in his sermons. We chose as our spokesman and head of the delegation an elderly person, Mr. Cristovão Furtado, who had perfect command of the Portuguese language, and who was a very persuasive talker. An interview with the chaplain was asked for and was granted. And then our delegation of three prisoners went and met him. Our spokesman did his job excellently. He assured the chaplain that the Indian people in general were a very religious people, that Nehru was a thorough democrat, and that in consequence India would never go Communist. And that being the case, we prisoners who were devoted to the cause of freedom, had felt hurt on being referred to in his sermon as tools of Communism. We were happy at the opportunity to hear mass every Sunday, but would Father in future avoid political subjects for his sermons?

The chaplain was really a good and pious man. I think he realised that as a priest his main concern was religion, and that there was no point in antagonising a congregation of prisoners whom he could otherwise serve as a minister of religion. He declared that he had no intentions of hurting our feelings, and he assured our delegation that there would be no politics in his preaching. And in fact we never had any further problems with him, nor any cause of dissatisfaction as long as he remained at Aguada.

30

AN UNLIKELY PRISONER

A Young Gentleman in Fine Clothes Lands into Prison

In the course of my prison life I came across different types of fellow prisoners representing a wide variety of human nature; and some of them were really interesting characters. The freedom struggle not only attracted full-fledged patriots, but it also drew into its vortex some very unlikely, out-of-the-way people, restless spirits and even some eccentrics. And some of these were very fine fellows – cheerful, generous and courageous. I particularly remember one such young man, who made a most dramatic entry into prison.

The corporal on duty or one of the guards under him used to open our cell-door at certain more or less fixed hours for various purposes like taking us out for fetching water, or handing in our provisions, or letting us out for a stroll. Hence most of the times when the door opened we guessed its purpose, and did not show much interest. But sometimes when the door was opened at odd hours, many of the prisoners would raise their heads and look towards the door with curiosity, trying to guess what the matter might be.

One fine day, towards noon, a guard unexpectedly came and unlocked the door with some urgency, and keeping it wide open stepped aside. Many of the prisoners watching with curiosity, thought that the Commandant of the fort or some important government official might be visiting our cell. But as we went on watching, a very astonishing sight appeared before our eyes. The corporal on duty entered with his most officious air, escorting a very unusual

Goan gentleman dressed like a diplomat in an expensive dark blue suit, wearing a most becoming felt hat, and carrying a handsome briefcase in his hand. For some time we were at a loss as to who the gentleman might be. He walked in with a most resolute step, and with a most self-confident look on his face, and then removing his hat with a grand sweep of his hand by way of salutation to us inmates, he bowed in front, he bowed to the right, he bowed to the left. And finally, as if getting into prison was for him the most natural thing in the world, he marched up with the utmost aplomb to the vacant bed indicated to him by the corporal, and began to make himself at home on his cot. I suppose, no one ever entered prison in such an impressive manner. Even the corporal and the guard seemed to be awed by the amazing gentleman.

We were all eager to know who the gentleman was, and how he landed into prison with all his fine clothes. His story which we gradually extracted from him after days of conversation, was as interesting as his unusual appearance.

He was the son of well-to-do parents, some landed proprietors of Salcete. He had lost his father early in life, but his mother having intended him for the Church, and at the same time wishing to give him good European education, had sent him to Portugal to join a seminary. But the young man had gradually begun to evince a trait on account of which he often got into scrapes: he developed an irresistible urge to engage himself in argument at the least opportunity, to dispute the most trifling proposition stated in his presence. (We had ample evidence of his argumentative nature during those months he was with us). On account of that little unfortunate prospensity he often got into verbal duels with the professors and superiors at the seminary, to the utter exasperation of the latter. I do not think he ceased to be a believer, but even then, he disputed the existence of God for the very pleasure of it, thus scandalizing all those ecclesiastical authorities. Finally, it appears, they decided that it was impossible for him to continue in the seminary, and they expelled him.

His expulsion from the seminary might have disappointed the mother, but not our hero, who immediately after was glad to join some law college in Lisbon, expecting to find the legal profession more conducive to his argumentative talents.

After studying for a year at the law college, he thought of spending some holidays with his mother at Goa. Accordingly he boarded the Portuguese steamer *Lurio* bound for Goa. Unfortunately for the former divinity student, there happened to be travelling by the same steamer a number of Portuguese military and police officers coming to assume duty in Goa. Inevitably, they began to talk about the situation in Goa, and, as could be expected they blamed Nehru's government for all the trouble in "Portuguese India." Our hero was not the man to allow their declarations to go unchallenged. He stoutly took up Nehru's defence and by implication cast slurs on the Portuguese regime – a thing which they must have never heard done in their life. They could not bear any criticism of their establishment, because tolerance was a virtue which was completely alien to men of Salazar's regime. As he described the situation to us: they really bristled with anger around him.

Having concluded that he was an "Indian nationalist," the officers took the assistance of the captain of *Lurio* and put him under a kind of house arrest in a cabin of the ship. And when the steamer touched Goa they handed him over to the police authorities, at the same time bearing testimony against him that he had spoken against Portuguese sovereignty in Goa. He was kept at police headquarters for a few days and closely questioned. I think the investigating officers finally realised that as far as they were concerned, he was only a harmless though irritating debater, and that it was not worth sending his case to the Military Tribunal for trial. They thought that instead, a few months' imprisonment at Aguada (the police had great powers) would teach him not to dispute Portuguese sovereignty in Goa. That is how after a few days' detention at Panjim he reached Aguada in all his fine European clothes. And the poor mother who was expecting the joyous arrival of the son, instead received a letter from him informing her that he had landed in prison. The poor old lady might have thought, what a come-down for her son: from the seminary to the law college, and from the law college to prison!

But he had no regrets: he felt himself quite comfortable in prison so long as he had people with whom he could engage himself in animated arguments. His sole pleasure in life seemed to be in argumentation. It was not at all safe to make a statement of a general nature in his presence; he would immediately throw you the gauntlet, and you would soon find yourself sparring with a formidable debater. But we all liked him: he kept us lively. And after a few months, when he was released, we missed him: our cell for some time wore a subdued air.

31

A GOAN POLICE CORPORAL IN PRISON

A Tragedy of Conflicting Loyalties

There were certain prisoners whose memories stand out with particular vividness in my mind because they were unusual in some way or the other. One such prisoner I often remember not only on account of his commendable conduct in prison (inspite of the fact that he had serious commitments outside and could not afford to remain in jail), but also because of the tragic fate which he met with outside after his release.

The man was a corporal in the Portuguese police, and, before he landed into prison, had been in charge of a police post in some village, with three or four constables under him. One night the post was attacked by a party of armed nationalists who after overpowering the corporal and his constables decamped with all the weapons and ammunition at the post. The corporal was then arrested for having failed to defend his post. In his statement to the police investigator he contended that he and his men could not defend the post as they were utterly taken by surprise by a large body of armed men, and did not have time to seize their weapons. But from certain information which he divulged to us, it appeared that he was a sympathiser of the freedom movement, that some of the nationalists who attacked the post were known to him, and that, in short, the surrender of the post was stage-managed by the corporal without the knowledge of his subordinates.

The police did not believe his story; they tried to extort from him the confession that he was in league with nationalists. But the corporal, inspite of being beaten stood by his story. So they could only charge him with dereliction of duty instead of treason. They suspended him from service and sent his case to the Military

Tribunal. For more than a year the case did not come up for trial; and in the meantime the poor corporal languished in jail while his wife and two or three children went through great hardships in the absence of any earnings from the husband. He worried about his family, yet somehow he pulled himself up and bore prison life bravely. We could see that he was patriotic at heart. He was confident that Goa would be free before long; and in jail he tried to prepare himself for that future by studying English assiduously, as he understood that in free Goa the Portuguese language would not have much importance. I have rarely seen people try to rise so determinedly above their present adverse circumstances and look with such confidence to the future, as he did.

Then after a year his case came up for trial. And contrary to his expectations he was acquitted by the Military Tribunal and released. We were all glad at his release because we knew that his wife and his children really experienced great suffering while he was in prison. It was only after a few months that we heard from some new prisoner the story of his tragedy.

On his being acquitted the police authorities had to reinstate him in service, and had to pay him the year's salary that had been held back. He had been then posted to take charge of a police post in another village. For some time life must have been comfortable for him and his family. But then tragic fate intervened again in his life. That police post was also attacked one evening by armed nationalists. This time his defence was immediate and vigorous (he was an energetic man). He must have thought in a flash that he could not bear once again the consequences of failing to defend his post. And he lost his life while defending it.

His lot was really tragic. By his sympathies he had been on the side of the freedom movement. But his life's circumstances – circumstances largely beyond his control – had placed him in a vulnerable situation in the opposite camp. He must have suffered considerably from these conflicting loyalties. And finally the tragedy had been clinched by the occurrence of the last unforeseen event – the attack on the police post – which was nothing but the work of a cruel fate.

But having lived in our midst for about a year he had endeared himself to us. We remembered him for the manly way in which he had tried to face misfortune, and for choosing in the end to die like a tragic hero.

32

THE GOVERNOR'S VISIT TO AGUADA

Another memorable event during those years was the visit of the Governor of Goa to the garrison and the prison of Aguada. General Vassalo e Silva who came to be much in the news at the time of liberation and after, had the honour and the misfortune to be the last Governor General of "Portuguese India" – honour because in his final hours as the Governor, he had the opportunity of doing some good to Goa; misfortune, because when Goa was liberated he was victimized by Salazar for having failed to defend Goa against the Indian armed forces, and a lot of obloquy was heaped upon him by the regime on that account. He had assumed the governor's office a few years before liberation, and within a short time he had succeeded in giving a more humane face to the Portuguese government in Goa.

We were informed of his visit by the corporal on duty, a few hours before his arrival, and we were asked to keep ourselves ready to receive him. None of us had seen him before, and at that time we knew little about him as a man. I was expecting to see in him the usual self-important, supercilious type of a military gentleman who would look down with scorn on us, political prisoners. But contrary to all our expectations he left a pleasant impression on us all.

We watched him with great curiosity as, accompanied by a number of military and government officials he entered our cell – an elderly gentleman dressed in a white uniform and bearing himself with great dignity. I remember how as soon as he stepped in, he looked carefully all over the cell, evidently to see in what conditions we lived. It was a fine gesture on his part; it prompted us to form a good opinion of the man. And then he walked slowly between the two rows of prisoners, observing us carefully, and stopping now and then to question a few prisoners who somehow roused his interest. He stopped in front of Mr. Pinto, one of our teachers from Aldona, who was standing next to me, and asked him, "Why are you in prison?" There was no harshness in his voice, it was almost gentle. And the teacher managed to answer in a tone in which there was neither submission nor defiance: "I am here because I want freedom for Goa." I watched the Governor's face closely to see how he reacted to that answer; it had no trace of anger, it remained quite impassive. He only nodded twice and then walked ahead.

We were surprised first of all that the Governor had deigned to meet us. His visit to the fort and the military garrison might have been in the normal course; but he could have gone away without seeing us prisoners. It was still more surprising that he had shown interest in us to the extent of questioning some prisoners about prison life, about their sentences, etc. Perhaps there was something unusual about the man, perhaps he was capable of rising above political differences and feeling sympathy for those who suffered, purely as a human being feeling for other human beings. I had seen great kindliness in the face of the man, and had felt sure that he had regarded us with some fellow-feeling. And in fact subsequent events at the time of liberation and after, proved that this good governor was capable of this kind of humanity.

His misfortune was the misfortune of a good man who comes to be a part of an evil system and who tries to resist it while being a part of it. The dictator Salazar, concerned only with the prestige of his regime, and probably in emulation of his Nazi and Fascist mentors, wanted General Vassalo e Silva to defend Goa at all costs – at the cost of the lives of all the Portuguese soldiers and not to let Goa fall without destroying it and leaving it in ruins. Governor Vassalo e Silva with his humanity and his good sense realised the futility and the cruelty of the dictator's plan. He was not prepared to sacrifice unnecessarily the lives of Portuguese soldiers in a suicidal battle against vastly superior forces. Nor did he have any relish for a senseless devastation which would bring loss and sorrow to innocent Goans. And for having surrendered without destroying Goa, he was charged with dereliction of duty and was humiliated by being stripped of his general's rank. For a decade and more he lived in disgrace. When we read in the newspapers, reports about his victimization, many of our freedom fighters remembering his visit to us at Aguada Prison felt sympathy for him in his ordeal. Having ourselves suffered under the oppressive regime we could understand the harrowing experiences he must have gone through all those years when he was vilified by Salazar's government and the controlled Portuguese press.

But finally fate proved to be kind to him in that it did not leave him to die in disgrace. The oppressive regime set up by Salazar was overthrown by the Portuguese armed forces, and the military regime which thus came into power reviewed his case. The new regime exonerated him from all the charges made against him, restored his full rank and all his honour, and completely rehabilitated him.

General Vassalo e Silva had a soft corner in his heart for Goans. When friendly relations were established between India and Portugal, he visited Goa, now as an old man, and was received with great warmth by the people here. It must have been something like a cathartic relief to him to visit Goa, which he must have always remembered as the place, where to his own peril, he had proved his humanity. Some years after this visit he died in Portugal, presumably, a happy man.

33

AN EPIDEMIC STRIKES AGUADA PRISON

During all those years of my life at Aguada, prisoners generally did not have great health problems. If there had been large-scale outbreaks of diseases like typhoid, or malaria or gastro-enteritis, the results might have been disastrous considering the congested conditions in which we lived. And how much medical care could we, enemies of the regime, expect from the authorities? But thank God, such a serious situation did not arise. Individual prisoners had minor ailments now and then, but we were fortunately spared, on the whole, affliction from serious illness – except once. Only once did we have a visitation of an alarming epidemic – the so called *Asian Flu*.

The notorious Asian Flu was said to have originated in Japan (hence the name Asian Flu), being caused by a new mutant virus. And from there, lodged within human bodies, it crossed seas and oceans, and swept all over the world ignoring national boundaries and political barriers. Before it reached India, I remember reading in the foreign newspapers, the influenza had assumed the proportions of quite an epidemic in a number of western countries. It was a very virulent kind of influenza; and in the colder countries of Europe it was reported to have taken a considerable toll of life.

Finally the epidemic reached Goa, and Aguada Prison. In our cell prisoners were attacked one after another and laid in bed with high fever, at once becoming weak and helpless. No remedy seemed to help much. The only thing that seemed to give a little relief was a steam bath from boiling-hot water infused with eucalyptus oil. We administered this remedy in the earlier stages to patients who had the strength to sit up in bed. But two or three days after the attack they had no strength to move at all. Besides, more and more people were attacked, till finally only about ten of us were left from a population of about fifty, to nurse all the others. Our cell began to resemble a hospital ward. I have never seen an influenza have such dreadful effects on people. For days, the sick lay motionless and with closed eyes like corpses; only now and then did they give out fearful moans. When we spoke to them they could hardly reply, speaking a word or two sometimes in weak whispers. Some of them seemed to be in such a terrible state that I was mortally afraid that those cases might prove fatal. Later, when they regained enough strength to speak, they told us how they had felt so weak that it had been an agony to move even a limb; and their minds were so clouded that they had to make a great effort to grasp what we were telling them.

Those who were not stricken worked untiringly for weeks nursing the sick with great care. Not all were so good at this work inspite of their concern and sympathy for the sick. I remember a few prisoners in particular who heroically rose up to the occasion and took the responsibility of caring for the sick mainly upon their shoulders. The rest of us also worked unceasingly, no doubt; but they were an inspiration to us because they worked without panicking, and with a sense of assurance. It was at that time I realised that only a few people are blessed with the magic touch of tenderly treating the sick.

But fortunately, one by one our sick recovered. About a month after the outbreak of the influenza, the last sick man in our cell was on his legs again; and the fearful epidemic – the Asian Flu passed off like a nightmare, leaving only its memories in the minds of those who had been its victims, and of those who had nursed them.

The epidemic was not confined to our cell alone. The other prison cells at Aguada also went through more or less similar conditions. Luckily there was no fatality in the whole of Aguada Prison, inspite of the fearful aspect in which the influenza showed itself. Perhaps it was dangerous only in cold regions.

34

EFFECTS OF PROLONGED PRISON STRESS

Long imprisonment had its adverse effects on the minds of prisoners. In this respect, it is difficult to say what types of natures can best stand up to the rigours of prolonged prison life. The very passage of years in prison does exert tremendous pressure on the mind of a prisoner – pressure which often results in mental depressions. And the unnaturalness of life in which the normal outlets to natural impulses are denied, builds up frustrations which sometimes threaten to unhinge the mind. No man, I suppose, can claim to have gone through a long period of imprisonment with complete equanimity, without his mind being subjected to assaults of depressions and frustrations. Sensitive natures naturally suffered more, but that is not to say that those natures necessarily suffered breakdowns. On the other hand, I have seen tough-looking people also suffer from various adverse effects of long imprisonment. I suppose it is mainly a question of inner adjustment, a question of mental resilience. Perhaps sensitive spirits with mental resilience could somehow fight off those depressions and frustrations and keep them at bay. Even so, it is difficult to say what exactly was lacking in those who developed symptoms of mental stress.

At different times we had five or six cases of prisoners showing symptoms of mental stress in varying degrees, ranging from the mild ones on the borderland of abnormality to the serious ones of complete mental breakdown.

Our earliest case was that of a prisoner who used to get terrible nightmares every third or fourth night. He had been beaten brutally at the time of interrogation and kept in solitary confinement for some months at police headquarters; and perhaps his nightmares were a consequence of those painful experiences. In the middle of the night he used to spring up from his bed, gesticulate wildly and shout and yell frightfully. I remember the first night of his nightmare particularly, when the other prisoners roused suddenly from their slumber, and frightened out of their wits by the horrible yells, had begun themselves to scream, without being aware of it. The terrible uproar thus produced in our cell had alarmed the sentries on the wall of the fort, and they had rushed down to our cell to investigate the cause of the uproar. Later, as we got used to his nightmares, we got up from sleep less with fear, but more with concern for his condition; and every time some of us would try to pacify him and put him to bed again. In the morning he did not remember anything of the fearful drama he had enacted in the night. It went on for months. But in this particular case there was gradual improvement in course of time. As his painful experiences at police headquarters receded into the past, they probably troubled him less and less. Besides the milder life at Aguada Prison together with the warm sympathy from a number of fellow prisoners must have had an ameliorating effect on his condition. His nightmares became less frequent, and after two or three years, as I remember, they ceased altogether.

There was another case of a prisoner, a middle-aged man, who was a victim of severe depressions. We noticed that gradually he became more and more morose and withdrawn. He began to sit most of the day on his bed with a fixed, vacant stare in his eyes, not taking interest in any activity. When we spoke to him he usually responded with a start, as if our call had jolted him out of his inner world. He also developed feelings of hostility particularly towards senior prisoners to whom he spoke with great irritation. But fortunately he remained friendly and genial to us youngsters, adopting an elder-brother attitude towards us. To keep him out of his depressions we tried to engage him in conversation, inducing him to talk about his participation in the 1946 movement about which he told us interesting anecdotes. This seemed to do him a little good. But some time later he had another misfortune – he lost a member of his family, which plunged him into grief and finally brought about complete nervous breakdown. He did not recover from it till his release which fortunately came a few months later. Then his recovery was complete; for when I met him after liberation he was quite normal.

Then we had a very tragic case. It was that of a very promising young man, a brilliant student of philosophy, a great idealist who had joined the freedom movement soon after graduating with honours at the Bombay University. He was hoping to resume his studies after fulfilling his patriotic obligation, after helping to win freedom for Goa. In the meantime he was thinking of keeping in touch with his subject by intensive reading. At police headquarters, where he had spent two or three months, he had experienced the usual police brutalities and then at Altinho prison, for being outspoken in his talk with an American journalist, he had been kept in solitary confinement for a couple of months. Perhaps he had found the loneliness of that life unbearable; perhaps it had been a real ordeal to him, an ordeal which had left its mark on his mind.

At Aguada prison, in the beginning, he seemed to be quite well. He read quite a lot, he discussed philosophy with us, and occasionally he wrote poems – some mystic type of poems. We were impressed by his eloquence and his vast knowledge. But after he had spent about a year at Aguada we noticed that though his talk continued to be fluent and brilliant, what he said was somehow divorced from reality. I, in particular, having held him in considerable esteem, was quite alarmed seeing his intelligent mind begin to lose touch with the world of reality. I remember myself remonstrating with him, earnestly appealing to him to take hold of himself and not to allow himself to disintegrate. But alas, that did not help, and we had to stand helplessly by and watch the cruel onset of insanity.

And then his reading stopped, his behaviour became more and more odd, his mind lost its balance. Though he continued to speak to us, we could see that he had lost all rational communication with us; his talk became more and more wild. And we who were his friends could do nothing to help him. We had as helplessly to witness the relentless march of insanity as we had watched its cruel onset.

He was taken to some government hospital; but whatever treatment was given there, did not seem to have helped him. (I wonder whether they had any effective psychiatric treatment in Goa in those days). And after being kept in hospital for some time he was released. But our unfortunate friend never found release from insanity. After liberation I met him sometimes. Though he recognised me and spoke to me, his talk was still irrational, his mind was still possessed with wild fantasies. He would wander from place to place, not eating proper food, not taking care of himself. And that might have brought about his early death.

It is one of the most bitter experiences of life to see a friend, a dear one with whom you always have had a meeting of minds, suddenly lose his mental equilibrium and slide into insanity; to find that his mind has receded utterly beyond the reach of your mind. The sense of helplessness, of frustration and of loss is tremendous. Many of us experienced that bitter feeling when our friend in prison suffered mental derangement and passed out of our life.

35

THE DECLINE OF THE FREEDOM MOVEMENT

Its Effects on the Prisoners' Morale

By the beginning of 1958 the non-violent movement in Goa had declined. The armed movement conducted by a number of groups had sputtered on a little longer, but by the middle of 1958 that too had ground to a halt. Goa had made a mighty effort to heave off foreign yoke with hundreds and hundreds of her sons joining the freedom struggle. It would be no exaggeration to say that almost every patriotic Goan had somehow been drawn into the fray, had somehow committed himself to the cause of freedom. Hundreds had courted arrest, filling all the jails in Goa,[1] and many after working underground, had crossed over into India going into voluntary exile. But the effort had not been enough to dislodge colonial rule. And Goa now seemed to lie exhausted and prostrate at the feet of its foreign rulers.

People from the rest of India had also come to our help. In 1955 hundreds of *satyagrahis* led by prominent political leaders like Madhu Limaye and N.G. Goray had marched into Goa from different directions. At certain places, only the leaders had been detained, the rest being assaulted and then immediately deported across the frontier. At other places the Portuguese troops had ruthlessly opened fire on the unarmed people, slaughtering many, and

1. [At the peak of the movement, there must have been about a thousand prisoners. But if we count all those arrested by the police and detained even for a short period, in connection with the movement, the total number of arrests must have been about three thousand.]

compelling the rest to withdraw. Since then the Indian government had again stopped Indian *satyagrahis* from entering Goa.

Even then it could not be said that the freedom movement was entirely dead when hundreds of patriots continued to be in jail: their very presence there, was a continuation of the movement. The Portuguese rulers could not go about their business with peace of mind when their jails were full of political prisoners. These congested jails were a constant reminder to them that they were unwanted in Goa. Further, the conscience of Goa and of the rest of India (to say nothing of the conscience of the world) could not rest easy when there were hundreds of Goan prisoners languishing in Portuguese jails.

But the above considerations were a poor consolation to prisoners who, with the decline of the movement, saw their goal of freedom for Goa recede into the remote future, and who now faced the more certain prospect of spending six, eight, ten or more fruitless years in jail. By the end of 1958 our hopes had ebbed to the lowest. There was now a perceptive change in the mood of prisoners.

A certain gloom seemed to descend upon Aguada Fort prison. Prisoners appeared to be more taciturn and dispirited. They still went about their daily routine but in a more mechanical manner, seeming to have lost their zest for all activity. Work which was formerly considered interesting seemed to have lost its charm and now appeared dull and stale; study seemed only a painful, futile effort; and even books appeared to have lost their power to enchant.

And while patriots thus languished in prison, life outside seemed to be going on smoothly, regardless of our anguish for the sake of freedom. From the windows of our cell we could get a view of the sea just in front of Marmagoa harbour, and there we used to see foreign ships brazenly entering Marmagoa port, and leaving it laden with iron and manganese ore for Japan and other countries. Those ships were probably unaware of the presence of political prisoners in the fort which they could see while entering and leaving the port. But we could not look at those ships which bolstered the Portuguese economy without being moved with indignation: Their uninterrupted arrival and departure seemed to represent the smooth functioning of the odious colonial regime.

With all quiet on the Goa political front we had the feeling that we were forgotten by the world, including our fellow Indians and fellow Goans. It was a demoralizing feeling, and in that demoralizing mood it was natural that our long sentences should weigh heavily on our minds. Though I wanted to keep away all gloomy thoughts by occupying myself in reading, I sometimes caught myself brooding over my future. In all probability, I was thinking, I would have to remain in jail till I completed my whole term of imprisonment, and that would be for another eight years. In that case all my youth would be wasted in jail; I would be more than thirty-two when I came out. What kind of life would I start at that age without much education, without having prepared myself for any career? And what if after twelve years of imprisonment I left jail broken in body and spirit?

Our minds were also troubled by a gnawing doubt whether all our sacrifices would bear fruit. Would those sacrifices move the Indian people and government to some effective action? Would the continued imprisonment of hundreds of Goans added to the martyrdom of tens of Goan and non-Goan Indian *satyagrahis* be a sufficient justification for the Government of India to take military action against Portuguese colonies? If not, Portuguese rule in Goa might last another decade or two, till Goans, after a respite of years – perhaps another generation of Goans – launched another struggle, a more powerful struggle to dislodge colonial rule. In that case our remaining in jail to complete the whole term of imprisonment was a near certainty.

36

TAPPING ONE'S INNER RESOURCES TO OVERCOME DEMORALIZATION

The end of 1958 and the beginning of 1959 was certainly a demoralizing period for prisoners with long sentences. But even in this demoralizing situation it was encouraging to note that prisoners did not give in to despair. They faced the situation grimly, but they faced it successfully, finding an inner strength to fight the demoralization. It is my conviction that in real grim situations one can tap unknown sources of power within oneself, sources whose existence one becomes aware of, if one does not easily give in to despair. And in the grim period of 1958-59, prisoners with long sentences could not have coped with the demoralization without drawing upon those inner sources of strength. My personal experience was that with some effort one could utilise those inner powers and go through very difficult situations with stoic fortitude; that one could, to a certain extent at least, be independent of external circumstances, and derive one's mental well-being chiefly from one's inner resources.

In March, 1959, I had completed four years in jail, and now I was trying to come to terms with the prospect of spending the rest of my sentence i.e. another eight years in prison. By then I had realised that I had to learn to live like a hermit in order to conquer the restraints of prison. I decided on a certain course of mental discipline. I set myself to plan how I would spend fruitfully those eight years or whatever period I had to remain in prison. I resolved to apply my mind once again to reading and to study.

And in a couple of months I had disciplined myself sufficiently to accept my situation, to instill a fresh sense of purpose into my life and to live with a new sense of direction. And I had every reason to be content with this little mastery of the spirit over external circumstances. For not only was I once again deriving satisfaction from ordinary activity and pleasure from books, but I began to experience at times, a peculiar sense of freedom, the kind of which I had never experienced before. It was quite a strange experience, and it will not be possible to give a clear idea of it.

I used to get this strange experience, not at all times of the day, but only in the evening at the time of sunset or a little later. Perhaps it had something to do with the peaceful, pensive mood induced by the quiet hour of sunset. At that time prisoners usually would relax after the little exertion of the stroll, before lighting their lamps and occupying themselves with something or the other. I had got into the habit of drawing myself away from all company at that hour, and sitting alone in a corner or at a window looking out at the evening shades spreading over the sea and then at the twilight creeping into the courtyard. At such times I would gradually drift into a reverie, with thoughts of home crowding into my mind.

It was some time after I had reconciled myself to the prospect of spending my whole term in jail that I began to experience, while sitting in reverie at the evening hour, a strange elation of the spirit, a sensation of being entirely free of all restraints. I was filled with an inexpressible sense of well-being in which the stone walls enclosing me did not seem to matter. Sometimes I would feel myself at home with my family, sometimes I would find myself transported to the haunts of my boyhood days, in the hills and forests around my village. At such times I would have a vivid, a clairvoyant's vision of the places in which I felt myself to be. It was a very joyful experience – an experience which convinced me that the human spirit could really triumph over the constraints of prison.

After the first few such experiences I tried to make it a daily practice to retire to a corner, or to a window at the sunset hour, to seek solitude in the midst of the crowded prison-cell, in pursuit of those precious moments of mental liberation; but many times I was disturbed by my fellow prisoners who broke in upon my solitude with their well-meaning talk, and thus deprived me of those valuable experiences. But whenever I had opportunities of going through those experiences, I found that they always fortified me, that they had a kind of transforming effect upon me.

37

THE GOVERNMENT HAS SECOND THOUGHTS ABOUT ITS CROWDED JAILS

Declares Partial Amnesty for Political Prisoners

We were not in truth forgotten. It was but natural that all those Goans and non-Goan Indians who had been in any way connected with, or had encouraged and sympathised with the Goan Freedom Movement should be seized with concern about the fate of hundreds of Goan prisoners wasting away in Portuguese jails. Consequently, various Goan organizations, as also a number of Indian political organizations were exerting pressure on the Government of India to liberate Goa and the other Portuguese-occupied territories without delay. The Government of India, on its part, was also anxious to solve the problem of Goa expeditiously. Nevertheless, Nehru's government was on the one hand averse to the use of force, and hence reluctant to take military action; and on the other, it was not prepared to allow Indian citizens to cross over into Goa after the massacre of *satyagrahis* by Portuguese troops on the Goa border in August 1955. In those circumstances the only course left open to it, was to try to put diplomatic pressure through certain countries on the Portuguese government, to make it surrender its colonial possessions in India. In pursuance of that course the Indian Government approached the governments of friendly democratic countries like Great Britain and the United States (which being Portugal's powerful NATO allies had considerable pull with it), urging them to use their influence with the Portuguese government to get it to vacate the Indian territories under its colonial occupation. Those democratic countries, while in principle sympathising with India's demand for the end of all colonial rule on its soil, were not eager to oblige India to the extent of putting pressure on Salazar's government. However, as a matter of ordinary diplomatic practice, the governments of those countries conveyed to the Portuguese government the purport of India's approach to them. The only reaction of the Portuguese government to this diplomatic move was, as could be expected, the intensification of the old stock propaganda that all Goans lived in great contentment under Portuguese rule, and that hence there was no Goan problem.

Of course it was difficult for the Portuguese government in these new circumstances to maintain that there was no Goan problem while all jails in Goa were full of political prisoners. Nor could this fact of hundreds of Goans being in jail be entirely concealed from foreign journalists, who, from time to time visited Goa. The government was anxious to present to all foreign visitors the appearance of a normal situation in Goa; and in this context, it was quite inconvenient for the government to have hundreds of prisoners in its custody.

By the middle of 1959 vague rumours began to reach us at Aguada Prison that the government was going to declare a partial amnesty for all political prisoners who had been sentenced for non-violent nationalist activities. Even if there was some truth in those rumours, we could not conjecture at first how far we would benefit from the amnesty. We thought perhaps one-third or even one-half of our sentence might be remitted by the partial amnesty; in which case only those prisoners who had been sentenced for short terms would get instant, tangible benefit; they would be entitled to immediate release. Whereas prisoners like me with long sentences, after the remission of one-third or even one-half of their sentence would still have to undergo years of imprisonment to complete their term.

It was some time later, some time after the proclamation of the amnesty that we got definite information about the government's scheme with regard to political prisoners. It was their plan to bring about the release of all non-violent prisoners and empty their jails, and with that end in view they devised the following strategem: they declared a partial amnesty remitting one-third of every non-violent prisoner's sentence; and they decided to release on parole all those who had completed half of their remaining sentence. Under this formula even prisoners with long sentences qualified for release.

It was a calculated move on the part of the government, and it was something of a gamble. It secured their objective of emptying their jails to create the appearance of political normalcy and stability in Goa. But there was a risk in hundreds of jail-released nationalists moving about outside: They might begin organizing fresh agitations against Portuguese rule. Here the government counted on the physical and moral exhaustion of prisoners who had spent four or five years of a hard life in jail. They felt confident that these tired men would not have the spirit to face the threat of years of imprisonment again. Moreover, they could keep a watch on the movements of all these known opponents of the regime, and in case of any suspicious activity on their part, they could haul them in, and, as their release was conditional, could detain them till the completion of their whole term without the trouble of fresh interrogation and trial.

38

RELEASE ON PAROLE

I Return Home After Four and a Half Years

We received this information of our early release on parole with mixed feelings. Naturally the thought that we would soon be out of prison made us glad. Whatever our principles and ideals, man, like his other fellow creatures, has a basic need of free physical movement; and the state of being shut up in a small, closed space is extremely unbearable to him. And so release from such a state of confinement was bound to give us great physical satisfaction. We were also happy that we could soon join our families from whom we had been separated so long. And finally many prisoners, especially those who had serious family responsibilities, felt glad that they could once again attend to their neglected domestic responsibilities and commitments.

But there was also regret in our minds that we were leaving prison without having completed the task which we had undertaken. At that time we were not fully aware how far our struggle had created the conditions leading to the final liberation of Goa – conditions particularly in the form of: (i) a world opinion favourable and sympathetic to the oppressed Goans; (ii) a roused Indian public demanding the elimination of colonial pockets on the national soil; (iii) an increasingly concerned Government of India, not only responding to the above two conditions, but also being moved by the sacrifices of Goans and committing itself to the liberation of Goa. But we were thinking of the unfinished struggle in terms of our Goans, and how our people at an opportune moment in the near future, could resume that struggle and carry it to its conclusion. We wondered to what extent during our imprisonment the Goan people were roused and made politically conscious by our struggle so far.

However, we knew the movement could not be revived immediately after our release because we were aware of our own exhaustion. We needed recuperation.

And then by the beginning of July 1959 prisoners began to be released from the various cells of Aguada prison, in groups of five or six per day. There were no means of knowing when one's turn would come; the corporal on duty would come and read a few names, then allow the prisoners a few minutes to get ready to leave prison. Day by day, week by week, our cell began to get emptier and emptier, till by the middle of August only about one-third of the number of prisoners were left. Finally on the 19th of August, 1959, came my turn for release. I hurriedly packed my things like books and clothes, in a wooden box, put on the only decent but old set of clothes I had with me, and after taking leave of the prisoners remaining behind (most of them expecting release) I walked out of Aguada Fort prison. After a few steps from the gate, I could not help looking back wistfully at the stupendous fort, now with long familiarity bereft of its terror – the fabled fort which had been my prison-home for three and a half years, and in which I had learnt to suffer and to endure.

Having lived in prison for four years and five months, I could not shake off the feeling of being a prisoner for quite some time after my release. On my way home from Aguada I first experienced this odd feeling: I fancied that the designation "prisoner" was stamped on my person, that I carried the air and smell of prison with me, and that people could easily mark me out as a "prisoner". I had got out of the habit of wearing outdoor clothes, and I felt that the set of clothes which I had taken out and worn after years of disuse ill-suited me and made me still more conspicuous as a prisoner. While travelling by *caminhão* from Aguada to Assonora I imagined that the other passengers were glancing at my clothes and then staring at me. And not only on my way home but even for some time after, I had a feeling that casual acquaintances as well as total strangers were looking at me with curiosity. It might have been all mere fancy on my part, but it did pose me a challenge to hold up my head as a former political prisoner.

All the way I was thinking of the excitement my sudden arrival would cause at home. My people had heard of the amnesty, they even knew that prisoners were being released, but as mine was a long sentence, they had not expected my release so soon. It was about four in the evening that I alighted from a *caminhão*, and proceeded towards our lone house by an unfrequented way. It is difficult to describe with what emotions I approached the dear old place where I had grown as a child and as a boy, and from which I had been taken away four and a half years ago; with what rush of feeling I caught a first glimpse of the house which now seemed to wear a deserted and forlorn look. I entered the verandah quietly and listened at the door which was ajar and I heard soft voices in conversation inside. Then I called out to my sister. There came from within two shrieks of joy in response – from my niece and my sister. Thereupon I pushed the door wide open and hurriedly strode in to embrace a sobbing mother.

And in the happiness of being re-united with my dear ones I forgot for some time all other concerns and anxieties.

39

AS A PAROLED PRISONER I FIND LIFE IMPOSSIBLE IN GOA

At Aguada, time had seemed to stand still, but outside, I became aware of changes indicating that the world was passing us by; that while we patriots thirsted for freedom and remained in jail, the world had gone on in its own way. Changes at home and in its surroundings impinged forcefully on my awareness right at the beginning. Many garden plants to which I was accustomed had disappeared and new ones had grown, some of them quite big, giving the garden an unusual appearance. Trees around the house which I had known as quite small had now become so big that I wondered when they had time to grow so much. The old domestic animals were no more, and in their place were new ones who took me for a stranger. All our neighbours also seemed to have grown unreasonably older.

All such changes, though they made me feel out of place, were not in any way painful, and I could adapt myself to them. But when I began to move out of the house I was faced with serious and painful changes which would make my life in Goa unbearable.

I found that most of those acquainted with me were unwilling to speak to me; even people who had been very friendly with me four and a half years ago now turned cold and avoided me: So much was their fear of being in any way associated with, even seen with a marked opponent of the regime. Only the old people of the village who had believed that I had been imprisoned for life seemed genuinely pleased that I had returned, and spoke to me with a little warmth and sympathy.

I also had to think of earning my livelihood; I was no longer a boy now, and I could not always go on being a burden to my family, who, even without me, found it difficult to manage with our slender resources. At the time of my release I had a vague intention of finding employment and remaining in Goa so that I might work for a further national awakening among Goans. But now I found that with my background of imprisonment it was very difficult to get any employment in Goa. Not even a private employer would risk incurring the wrath of government authorities by employing a marked enemy of the regime.

As I was released on parole, I was in quite an uncomfortable position, being watched over by the local police, and having to present myself once a fortnight at the Mapusa police station. At the time of release I had not thought much of those constraints, but now finding myself rendered idle and useless by all the cramping conditions of life in Goa, my spirit rose in revolt against the restraints placed upon my freedom. I thought I would not submit to the indignity of presenting myself at the Mapusa police station. A fortnight passed after my release, but still I did not go and report at the police station, inspite of knowing that the consequences of that act of omission could be serious.

Though I was happy in the midst of my family in those days after my release, I could not for long ignore that I was living in a precarious situation. In about twenty days I fully realised that it was impossible for me to stay in Goa. It was a painful realisation because, apart from my great desire to remain in Goa to serve the cause of freedom, I was unwilling to part again so soon from my family after the recent separation of four-and-a-half years.

40

ESCAPE FROM GOA

My Solitary Flight Across the Border

Twenty days after my conditional release I decided to escape from Goa and go to Bombay. Most of the leaders of the movement, including Peter Alvares were in Bombay, and a number of our released prisoners also, as I learnt, had escaped and gone there. I intended to meet and consult them to find out whether they had any plan of action in which we could participate. And if there were no possibilities of the movement being revived early, I thought, I would attend to matters concerning my personal development. Though more than five years had elapsed since I passed the S.S.C. examination, I still cherished the ambition of taking higher education and preparing myself for some career.

Once the critical decision was taken, I was in a hurry to leave Goa. As I had not presented myself at the police station, I was afraid that I might be summoned and detained, or that my movements might be watched in such a way as to foil my attempt at escape. Even then, separation so soon from my family being quite painful, I delayed my departure a bit, and spent another two joyful days at home; and then putting some clothes and a few other necessary things in a small cloth bag, and taking a small amount of money given to me by my sister, I prepared myself to depart. I did not know when I would see my family again, because, so long as the Portuguese ruled Goa, I could not return except on pain of being arrested and imprisoned again for eight years. Nevertheless, I promised to come and see them secretly (though they were against my taking that risk) about a year after establishing myself in Bombay.

A little after nightfall I bade farewell to my dear ones, and cautiously left the house with the bag slung over my shoulder and a stout stick in my hand. It was a dark night, which was to my advantage, because being all alone, I felt more secure in not being seen at all. Presently I passed beyond the outskirts of the village and gained the safety of the hills. And then I began the long, solitary night-march through hills and forests to the Sanquirvale frontier. My progress was quite slow, as, it being the end of the rainy season, the grass on the hills had grown tall, and the bushes were thicker with leaves and creepers. Having undertaken a number of times the journey by this same route five years before, I was confident of steering myself in such a way as to avoid the forest villages that lay along this route. Not that there was any fear of the police in those remote villages; however it would have been extremely awkward for a lone traveller to stumble into one of them in the middle of the night and rouse all the dogs and alarm all the men in it. All the same, I cannot say that my mind was free of all apprehensions as I set out alone in the dark on this eight-mile journey through wild terrain. I had, for instance, a little fear of a chance encounter with some dangerous wild animal, but I accepted all such fears as inescapable concomitants of such a journey.

However, as I trudged on and on without any mishap past some of those hamlets now lying quietly asleep, I forgot my fears, and began thinking instead of the dismal nature of the present journey. I saw it in constrast with those exciting journeys I used to undertake along with groups of other nationalists, five years before in the heyday of the freedom struggle. With what enthusiasm and hope had I then led batches of eager young patriots across the frontier for meetings with leaders of the movement! And with what confidence in the ultimate triumph of our cause had we returned from each meeting to intensify the freedom movement! Now, after five years of a hard struggle here was I, a lonely fugitive, running away in the dark from my own land, not knowing when I would return to it. And instead of an invigorating enthusiasm, I was feeling now only a benumbing fatigue, instead of confidence in the early triumph of our cause, only a forlorn hope flickering in my breast. The very thought that my journey was nothing but an escape caused me pangs of regret. Like every released prisoner I felt myself irrevocably committed to the cause of freedom by the sacrifice of valuable years of our life; and now it looked as if I was fleeing from that commitment.

Agitated by these thoughts of regret I walked on like one in a daze, regardless of all danger. And then with weary steps at midnight I approached the frontier which had to be crossed with the utmost caution. It had been our old practice to stop a furlong or two before crossing the frontier, and while resting our weary limbs, observe and listen for any signs of danger. But now I was in such a perturbed state of mind as to be oblivious of all danger. Now I sat on the ground maybe partly from force of habit, but more from a desire to sort out my thoughts and reconcile myself to my flight, before I stepped out of my land.

I told myself that this escape could not be helped, that anyhow by escaping I was not abandoning the cause; in truth I could not abandon it, as that would render all my past sacrifices meaningless and futile. I promised myself that whenever the necessity for our services arose, I would make myself available for the cause in whatever situation I might be, whether now, or in the future. I reminded myself how a number of men who had taken part in the 1946 movement and had even suffered long imprisonment, had again found within themselves the will and the courage to plunge in the struggle when the 1954 movement began. I thought that it might be our destiny too to wage a second struggle in the 1960's. Sitting there a couple of furlongs from the frontier, alone in the middle of the night, I firmly resolved to be ready to answer whenever the country called again.

Then feeling myself strengthened by that resolve I rose up and unhurriedly advanced towards the frontier. I did not feel like hurrying away even on crossing the Portuguese frontier-road. After walking about a hundred meters from it, I stopped and turning round cast one long, last look at the dear land that I was leaving for the first time in my life. But except for the indistinct smudges of the nearest bushes, nothing could be seen of the landscape in front, in the murky darkness that enveloped the earth. Only from above came a faint glimmer of light from the stars visible through a few openings in the cloudy September sky.

I could not linger long at the frontier being called away by the unfinished journey – a journey which was leading me into a future as obscure as the surrounding gloom. I turned my back on Goan territory, and with a heavy heart directed my steps to the village of Sanquirvale where I intended to surrender myself to the customs authorities.

EPILOGUE

In Bombay, I found that we who had come after being released from prison could hardly do anything to serve the cause of Goa's freedom. We met the leaders of the movement and had discussions with them, we attended various meetings called by different political organizations; but no plan to revive the struggle was forthcoming[1] We could sense among all the Goan patriots in Bombay the same exhaustion of spirit that we ourselves were experiencing. The feeling among most nationalist circles there was that Goans had done their utmost to prove to the world their yearning for freedom from colonial yoke, and that it was high time for the Government of India to come to their rescue. Many nationalists were of the view that now the most important task for Goan political organizations was to mobilize Indian public opinion to demand of their government an immediate solution to the Goan problem. Some of them assured us that the Government of India was already urgently exploring every avenue to find a peaceful diplomatic solution to the problem, failing which, it would be compelled to resort to armed intervention.

In the circumstances, there was nothing for me to do except watch the situation and wait in patience. In the meantime I thought of attending to my personal development which had been neglected all these years. To support myself in Bombay, I procured some employment, and took admission in a college, thus resuming my education after a lapse of seven years. But it was only with half a heart and half a will that I could attend to personal matters. The mind remained constantly preoccupied with thoughts of the uncompleted task, the unfulfilled responsibility. The struggle for

---

1. [Our National Congress (Goa) and the other organizations of Goans had united themselves under the Goan Political Convention which while exploring the possibilities of re-starting the struggle, also tried to move the Government of India to solve the Goan problem].

Goa's freedom had become so much a part of our life that there was no ease for our restless spirit until the goal of that struggle ws reached.

Then with great jubilation we received the news that the Indian army was marching into Goa. And Portuguese colonialism which had thrived for four and a half centuries, had seemed to be so solidly entrenched on Indian soil, and had appeared to many people to be part of an eternal order of things, suddenly collapsed in two days.

It is impossible to give an idea of the thrill of joy that we patriots experienced on the liberation of Goa – on finding that the cause for which we had sacrificed years of our life was victorious; that the goal of freedom which at one time had seemed so remote was now finally realised. And along with joy came a tremendous sense of fulfilment that our sacrifices had borne fruit, a great sense of relief that our mission was accomplished.

Another matter of satisfaction for us was the fact that the liberation of Goa was effected with the minimum loss of life. For fourteen years India had patiently tried to find a peaceful solution to the problem of Portuguese colonies in India, but to no avail; in the last resort it was compelled to liberate those colonies by means of military action. Though there was the use of force, it was gratifying for us who had waged the non-violent struggle, to note that this was one of the least bloody military operations in history, considering the importance and magnitude of the action. The reason why there were so few casualties on both sides was that the whole operation was conducted by the Indian armed forces with discipline and with a sense of regard for human life.

With the liberation of Goa, many of us thought that our responsibility to our land, which we had assumed while joining the freedom movement, was over. But some felt that our land still needed our services, and that we could best serve her by providing the Goan people with political leadership, particularly in the transition period after liberation. As for me, I found that I had no political ambitions, that public life held no attraction for me. Rather, I thought that the most pressing task before me at this juncture of my life was to acquire some education, prepare myself for some career and stand on my own legs. Hence I decided to stay on in Bombay to continue my college education.

And like me a large majority of freedom fighters, considering that their obligation was at an end with the coming of freedom to Goa, decided in favour of their personal and family responsibilities, and remained out ot politics. It was only later when political conditions quite contrary to our expectations developed in Goa, that many freedom fighters came to regret their decision to remain out of politics – a decision which in the circumstances at that time they could not help taking.

Most of us who plunged into the freedom struggle in 1954 were young idealists who envisaged for free Goa an almost perfect state of affairs, something perhaps like the 'heaven of freedom' visualized by Tagore in his poem "WHERE THE MIND IS WITHOUT FEAR." As we were inexperienced idealists, this ideal of ours was inevitably vague, but lofty enough to sustain us through the struggle and through imprisonment. So it was but natural that the kind of political situation that finally came to prevail in Goa should have made us feel that it was a betrayal of our ideal. Not only we, but many other Goans felt that things could have been far better in Goa if the freedom fighters had remained as a cohesive force after liberation and had provided the necessary political leadership, and served the territory with the same zeal and energy with which they had participated in the freedom struggle.

The freedom fighters, at least a section of them, did make an attempt in the beginning to provide that political leadership. After liberation, many of the senior freedom fighters organised the Indian National Congress in Goa, and in the first assembly elections sought people's mandate to serve Goa. Most of them were patriots of proven integrity, being tempered by years of imprisonment, and the Congress party which they then represented enjoyed much credit in India and abroad, as it was then led by Jawaharlal Nehru. But it was the Goan electorate that at that time let down the freedom fighters. Swayed by narrow loyalties, by and large they opted for regional-communal parties. And the result of this political immaturity on the part of our electorate has been that since then we have been getting the kind of governments which, in a way, we have deserved. Rather too late the Goans woke up to the benefits of government by the national-secular Congress party. But alas, it was not the same Congress as in the days of Nehru. In Goa, most of the freedom fighters, who had organized the Indian National Congress, after the set-back at the first elections, gradually dropped out of active politics and began to attend to their personal lives, which in the case of many lay largely in ruins; and the Congress ranks, before the party came into power, were swelled by opportunists and careerists in politics. It was undeniably a lamentable situation that the freedom fighters, who, with their proven patriotism and their background of sacrifices would have been better qualified to serve this territory, could not much influence the course of events in Goa after liberation.

The plaint voiced by many of our patriots, and by other people besides, that the freedom fighters should have remained together as a cohesive force and given this territory "a good government" ignores the question as to how many of them, particularly after the electoral setback, could afford to sacrifice more years of their life, when most of them had already sacrificed five to ten years in the freedom struggle. Many of the senior freedom fighters had already given up their jobs and careers to join the freedom movement; some had left off their business, or their trade, or their farming; some of the younger ones had sacrificed their education. And now after liberation, if they were to provide Goa with political leadership, the sacrifice that was required of them was years of patient work among the Goan people to win over their confidence, and years of privations that the sincere pursuit of such work would entail. Most of our freedom fighters were simply not in a position to make this another sacrifice.

In a way it was better that most of us remained untouched by practical politics because we were also spared its vitiating influence. As freedom fighters, our goal had been the freedom of Goa, and we are grateful that fate vouchsafed us the achievement of that noble goal.

Not that we are the same naive idealists that we were when we joined the movement. Life has taught us to be more pragmatic. Now we realise that a perfect state of affairs is not possible anywhere. It is a part of the tragedy of human existence that great ideals get tarnished in the very process of realization. Under the best of conditions, with the best of men trying to translate their dream into reality, the reality, alas, always falls far short of the dream. And what can we expect in politics with its proverbial corrupting influence on men?

And yet idealism is needed, for without idealism life degenerates into shameless self-seeking. Only idealism, I believe, can help to regenerate society now and always. A great many people of my generation, moved by idealism fought for Goa's freedom. Perhaps the memory of their struggle will help to kindle idealism in another generation. Perhaps in the near future idealism will regenerate a Goan society which will tolerate as its political leaders only men of character, men with a spirit of service.

INDEX